TIME BEFORE THE MAST

Ivan Hazelton

CHAFFCUTTER

First Published 2001
The first edition was digitally printed 'on demand' and published by Minerva Press,
shortly before they ceased to trade - very few copies are believed to have been produced.

This fully revised edition published by
Chaffcutter Books
2003

ISBN 0-9532422-5-0

Chaffcutter Books, 39 Friars Road, Braughing, Ware, Hertfordshire SG11 2NN, England

Printed and bound in Great Britain by
Piggott Printers Limited, The Paddocks, Cherry Hinton Road, Cambridge CB1 8DH, England

TIME
BEFORE
THE
MAST

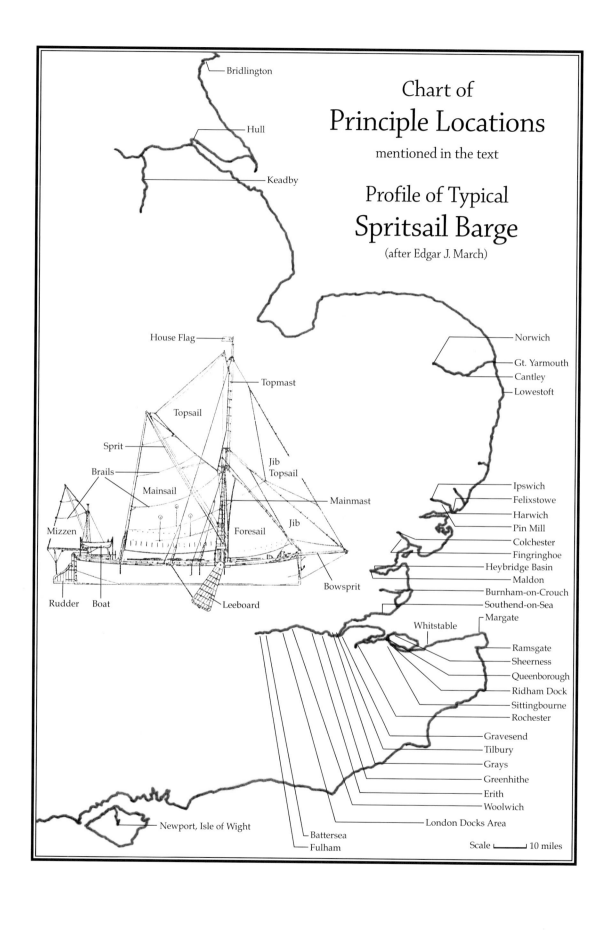

Chart of
Principle Locations
mentioned in the text

Profile of Typical
Spritsail Barge
(after Edgar J. March)

Bridlington

Hull

Keadby

House Flag — Topmast

Topsail

Sprit

Jib
Topsail

Brails

Mainsail

Mainmast

Jib

Mizzen

Foresail

Bowsprit

Rudder   Boat

Leeboard

Norwich

Gt. Yarmouth
Cantley
Lowestoft

Ipswich
Felixstowe
Harwich
Pin Mill
Colchester
Fingringhoe
Heybridge Basin
Maldon
Burnham-on-Crouch
Southend-on-Sea
Margate

Whitstable

Ramsgate
Sheerness
Queenborough
Ridham Dock
Sittingbourne
Rochester

Gravesend
Tilbury
Grays
Greenhithe
Erith
Woolwich
London Docks Area

Newport, Isle of Wight

Battersea
Fulham

Scale └──────┘ 10 miles

ABOUT THE AUTHOR

Ivan Hazelton was born in 1929 and grew up and lived in the dockland area of Ipswich. As a youngster he was a keen student of the spritsail sailing barges. His father had started out in one, and one of his grandfathers was a blue water sailor, lost at sea in a square-rigger.

From an early age he learned much about the barges, their rig and cargoes. As a Sea Scout, Ivan managed to get afloat most weekends. Then, just before his fourteenth birthday, he was able to sign on as third hand of a sailing barge. It was the middle of the 1939 to 1945 war and work was aplenty. From a very young age he had assumed a career afloat - this was his choice, and the sea his provider. He passed through sail and power, had a very brief time shore-side as a brewer's drayman, and then went back to sea.

Another twenty-one years passed before he thought about a life on land again, swallowing the anchor after twenty-five years at sea.

In recent years Ivan and I just sailed about in our yacht, the *Swin Ranger*, a fine long-keeled Bermudan sloop, just to enable him to keep his hand on the helm. Wintertime weekends were sometimes spent out after the elusive local whiting and cod in the nearby fishing grounds.

He looked forward to a long retirement with the freedom to do as his inclination prompted, and the pages penned by him which follow are a testimony to that philosophy and his lifelong love of the sea.

Sadly the results of this labour were not to be enjoyed by Ivan, for he passed away just before the production of his book was complete. Ironically, his publisher went out of business shortly after, and very few copies of the first edition went on sale. This new edition from Chaffcutter Books is a fitting tribute to the author's life.

Pam Hazelton
Ipswich
2003

CONTENTS

Ipswich Dock, with Cranfield Brothers' *Spinaway C* deep laden under the grain elevator.

Chapter I
A THOUGHTFUL TRIO

Us three lads gazed wishfully through the dark and dirty waters of the Ipswich dock, doing our usual thing of trying to capture eels from around the dolphins[1] at the Eagle Mill. Each had a ball of wool with worms threaded down part of the wool, and inside the ball a small weight. The object was to lower the ball of wool with its worms into the water, hoping that the eel, going for the bait, would get its teeth caught in the wool. The method had been known to be very effective.

Nibs and Ray, who were brothers, and myself were very good friends. Nibs and me, although only about nine years old, were always talking about the sailing barges. Even at that early age we had already picked up quite a lot of knowledge about the hulls and rigs of these craft and had even started to get to know some of the bargemen. Nibs and Ray came into contact with quite a few, more than did at this time, as their father kept a public house near enough on the dockside, the crews frequently dropping in for their pints.

It was there we met one old gent, Mo King, who was mate of the *Thalatta*. He had previously been in sailing boomie barges[2] and steamboats. Old Mo gave them great encouragement, naming parts, teaching them all the essentials a third hand should know, including how to scull a boat. This was really the introduction to the apprenticeship that I was later to serve. Old Mo was also a great teacher of seamanship and explained how to cope with problems as well as everyday things. The knowledge imparted by Mo King was to be of great use as time went on, but it was also going to get the three of us into trouble.

Nibs, Ray and I were again kicking our heels around the ship and barge repair yard one day. Stones were skimming across the river as we three were trying to see who could achieve the greatest number of dimples on the water. In our line of vision was the old bucket dredger moored about two hundred and fifty yards from the shore.

One or other of us suggested that the dredger would be a good place to investigate, and we agreed that it was to be our objective. We first searched the yard area to try and find something to get afloat with, but all to no avail. There were no craft in the yard being repaired at this time, so we would not be able to borrow a barge's boat.

The days passed by, but we did not waiver in our determination to get out to the dredger. We at last agreed that an old boat lying on the shipyard

[1] Mooring posts, or anchored spars with mooring rings, and latterly more substantial timber mooring structures. [2] Gaff rigged ketch barges with bowsprits.

foreshore would have to do, even though she had a couple of nasty holes. We were determined to repair her and that she would become our tender. This was the first time that we thought about using our initiative and old Mo's ideas on repairs. We would use brown paper and tar, with wood from the boat's floorboards being used for the final outside patch.

After a few evenings our dreams and repairs had become reality, we were ready to fulfil our mission to get out to the old bucket dredger. And so our first launching took place, in we got and off we set. At that time the only means of propulsion was for a couple of us to paddle using pieces of flooring, the other trying to steer with another piece hanging over the stern. Our repairs were not very successful and our boat began to leak alarmingly. We managed to get back to the beach and then held a 'council of war' to decide on our next move.

After lengthy deliberation we decided that we would have to apply pitch to the inside of our repaired areas. We had a look around the shipyard to see what we could find and came across some of their blocks of pitch. We managed to break off enough for our job. Melting it down took some ingenuity but at last we managed it. We were then able to run the hot pitch down over our patches to make them more watertight and the poor old boat a bit more serviceable.

Our next launch was a great success and not a drop of water came in through our patches. It taught us one very valuable lesson – never cut corners when repairing boats, particularly when water has to be kept in its place. It was a lesson well learnt at our tender years.

At last we were able to get out to the dredger. It was great fun to give it a real going over. We were able to climb from bucket to bucket and have a really exciting time out there, but alas our fun was short lived.

We had been out to 'our dredger', as the bucket tub was now known to us, for our fourth trip. As we boarded it, Alfie, the Mate of one of the sailing barges moored to a set of buoys close by, gave us a hail. He told us that we were being watched from the pier heads, and also the police had been told to watch out for us. Being the lads we were, nothing could have shaken or frightened us in those days, so very little notice was taken of him.

But our friend Alfie, sadly to say since drowned, was correct and we went ashore after about our sixth trip straight into the arms of the law. We were for the high jump for sure! After much garbled lecturing by the police, we were given our first courtesy ride. It is true to say that the three of us were very much down in the dumps after the police had so kindly given us our lifts home. First, they dealt with my two mates who lived in their pub not very far from where we were picked up. The senior policeman went in with them and after what seemed like eternity my turn came. I was also driven home in style. In those days just seeing a car in our road was an event, and there were all kinds of gasps from the mums on the street. As it was a warm day they were having their customary gossip, sitting on their front window sills. My arrival with a police escort, in front of her friends and neighbours, was not very popular with my mother. The policemen had a long talk with her.

After they had departed, and although my father had yet to return from work, came the first of my hidings. That was bad enough, but the worst punishment was not being allowed out 'until we see what the law does.'

Well we didn't have long to wait for their decision, for it came from the owner of the boat that we had repaired. He was the landlord of another pub called The Vine. The only charge that could be brought against us was the alleged stealing of his oars which, of course, we had never seen. At the Magistrate's Court the old bugger even praised us for the repairs we had done to his boat and for making it into a seaworthy craft. However, the so and so still persisted with the story that we had his oars, and we were duly fined the heavy sum of ten shillings (50p). We had also to suffer the stigma of two years' probation.

My poor old mate Nibs promptly passed out and had to be revived. His brother Ray said he would never have anything more to do with the sea, and as far as I know he never did. Nibs and I still carried on giving a helping hand to the bargemen with their dock work, learning more of their way of life as we did, and one day we were to be amply rewarded for our interest.

Thalatta, with *Gravelines I* ahead of her, both empty and under power in the London River.

Chapter II
A GALE IN THE S'TH'RD

It was to be a particularly great morning for us lads. It was a Saturday, and Nibs and I used to do a coke round. The coke run, as we used to call it, was really taking our old prams to the houses around our area to see if the folks wanted any coke from the gas works. If they did, we would go down and fetch it. The bag would cost them a tanner ($2^1/_2$ p) and the most that we could expect for getting it was something like tuppence. The run was about a mile there and back so the money was well earned.

It was whilst we were going down to the gas works that particular Saturday that we ran into old Mo. Ipswich millers R. & W. Paul's barge *Thalatta* was lying down at the docks alongside the Eagle mill. She was due to sail at about 10.30 that morning. Mo said that if we were aboard by then, we could have a trip down river as far as Pin Mill.

The old pram certainly flew along for the rest of that run. I'm afraid the remainder of our customers had to go without their coke and we lost quite a few who we were never able to regain. At the time we couldn't have cared less. We were off aboard a barge, and nothing was going to stop us.

There must have been more than half an hour to spare when we arrived on board, for they hadn't started to lock in arriving craft which would enter before we could leave. Mo said we should have a good cup of strong tea before we went any further, and so we did. Thick and laced with full cream condensed milk and brown sugar sweepings.

Ted finally arrived with his little motor tosher[1] alongside. He informed Captain Ruffles that as it was blowing so hard, he would only be able to take him to the end of the quay, Hog Island as we used to call it, where the Cliff Quay power station was later built.

The first job we had to do was to pass the tow rope out through the starboard 'snatch'[2] and then back past the bowsprit shrouds. We were then able to pass the rope by hand to Ted. After placing the eye over his towing hook he was able to take the strain. Then it was jump about shore side and let go of all ropes. Gradually and slowly he was able to pull us clear of the mill.

Once the short run from the berth to the lock was over and we had locked in, we had a short spell to wait before the water in the lock was level with the river outside and the outer lock gates could be opened so the *Thalatta* could pass through. Whilst the barge was waiting we were not allowed to stand

---

[1] A powerful launch used for towing and general duties. [2] Iron fairlead (in this context).

about. Old Mo kept us busy coiling down mooring ropes and then lashing down everything including spars and ropes upon the hatches.

At long last Nibs and I sort of looked at each other and, without a word being said, just grinned. By then Ted's tug had again taken the strain and we were off.

Nibs and I were still not allowed to relax, for Mo had let go the clewlines to the topsail, and having pushed the topsail sheet[1] into our hands, was heaving the head of the topsail up clear to take the weight off the head-stick. Pulling that sheet out was a lot more than Nibs and I could do, but soon old Mo had joined up with us and with a bit of an old shanty from Mo we soon had the sheet out to the sprit[2] end. Then it was up with the head of the sail. As this job was done with the aid of a winch we were able to manage this between us, but as soon as it was up I think we were both ready to collapse.

Before we could get our second wind, there came a roar from Captain Ruffles to hook the mainsheet block onto the traveller and get the mainsail set. This proved to be a hairy time for Nibs and me. Mo, who was built like an ox, had grabbed hold of the block which, as the wind was in the loose foot of the sail, was flying about quite a bit. I doubt if Nibs and I could even have lifted the block at that time. Old Mo was also shouting instructions to us to let go lowers and middles, and then it was let go the main brails[3], until the mainsail was finally sheeted home. Next we released the gasket from the foresail, a job we youngsters could cope with. Shortly after came the roar from aft, 'Let go the tosher!' The rope was cast off by the tug and was duly hove aboard as it flowed to the bow, the way Mo had told us it would. It was soon coiled and stowed. Coming from aft, another roar, 'Set the foresail!' but Mo was already there.

Soon after, the Captain bore away and we were off. The roar of the wind in the rigging was the only sound we could or wanted to hear at that time. After standing about a bit, we began to realise that we had both got very cold.

Our peace was to be short lived. The roar came again from aft, 'Ready about!' and Mo told me to stand by the foresail bowline[4], and I jumped to it just to get warm. The next shout was, 'Lee ho!' and as the Captain spun the wheel the *Thalatta* came through the wind, the foresail was soon aback, and the old girl flew round. The next shout was, 'Let draw!' and the barge gained speed on the new tack. I then walked down to leeward and passed the bowline through the foresail cringle ready for going about again.

Mo decided that Nibs and I would change jobs after a couple of boards[5] so now it was my turn to have a go at the leeboards[6]. What a job that proved to be. As the barge came into the wind you dropped the board that was to be the lee one and then wound up the windward one. The short boards that we were making meant that I was fully occupied and well shattered before we had got very far.

[1] Ropes to control sails. [2] Pronounced 'Spreet', a diagonal spar supporting the peak of a sail. [3] Main, middle, lower and peak brails are ropes used to furl spritsails. [4] Rope to hold foresail aback to help barge to turn through the wind. [5] The bargeman's term for tacks, by which the barge can travel against the wind. [6] Pivoting oak boards lowered to prevent leeway.

We arrived at Pin Mill. As it was our first sail in a barge it was the one that we would never forget. After we dropped anchor at Pin Mill old Mo had to go aloft to make a 'harbour stow' of the topsail. We lads were trying to make some sort of a job of the foresail and Captain Ruffles gave us a few harsh words before we had given him the 'harbour stow' that would satisfy him.

He then flew off into a small rage, as Mo termed it, to prepare himself for the shore. Very soon he let it be known that he was ready for the land. Very rapidly the riding lights were set up, and as everything was now snug, Captain Ruffles said, 'Right, now let's away home.' So it was into the small boat and pull for the shore. After a nice pull up along the land we finally made it to the hard.

As old Mo lived ashore at Pin Mill he was soon going to be home. After we had walked to the top of the hill and were at Chelmondiston, we came to the pub called the Red Lion. This was where Mo was going to leave us. He gave Nibs and me a shilling each and bid us bon voyage. When the Ipswich bus came along Captain Ruffles and we lads boarded it and the Captain paid our fare as well as his own. We were well happy as the journey's conversation all the way home was about the barge.

On that day I vowed to Captain Ruffles that one day I would be a barge master. He said he didn't think that there would be many craft left even though at that time only about half a dozen or so local barges had an engine, so there were still plenty under sail.

At that time, with my heart having become set on going to sea, I found that at my young age the nearest that I was going to get was to join the Sea Scouts. I never regretted it and will be forever grateful to Mr Hawkes, the Skipper, who eventually became Acting District Commissioner many years later. The effort he put into teaching us lads could never be repaid, except by our determination to succeed.

After joining and progressing through the basics of tenderfoot and second class, I had to make sure that I could swim twenty-five yards fully clothed, and then undress in the water. This was a condition that had to be met before we were allowed afloat. Once this milestone was achieved I thought I would be allowed afloat all the time, but this was not so. I soon found out that the only way I was going to get afloat regularly was to volunteer for the working party, so that was my aim.

I had to hastily cram for a full boatman's badge. The rowing and single sculling were all right, as I had learned these skills in my dock work with the barges. I then had to learn to sail a gig on my own. This turned out to be easier than I thought, and led in turn to my boatman's badge.

After this, a spell of sailing on my own to gain experience was required before I was judged proficient to teach some of those less fortunate than me. Even then, the rota system only allowed us to get afloat about one weekend in six. Our gigs were, as a matter of interest, given to the Sea Scouts by the sailing vessel *Joseph Conrad* when owned by Alan Villiers.

As time went on I was soon to learn that to get afloat every weekend called for drastic measures. The only way forward was to offer my services to the Skipper to work in the galley. This was one of the few berths that was always becoming vacant. I therefore became a regular.

After a period of about six months I had really begun to enjoy galley work. I considered that the experience would be valuable, as my first job had to be as third hand in a barge. This really meant cook, deckhand and general dogsbody. However, I then had a long way to go as a cook. Still, the weekends came and went during which I was taught the basic elements of cooking, and especially how to use a coal range. The day came when I was able to master the old favourite of sultana duff plus the roast joint and a few other basic recipes.

I was enjoying life to the full, for between cooking there was plenty of sailing and rowing. As well as doing my galley duties I was also by this time 'master of the galley'. This meant that I had more free time as somebody else did the chores such as peeling the spuds, the washing up and such like.

Only another year and oh, how the time did drag. The day eventually came when I could say that I had to look for a berth. As it was the middle part of the Second World War berths were quite easily come by. The pay for third hand was only £1. 18s. 0d. (£1.90) per week, and four pence of this was to pay for the stamp. The cost of the food was divided equally between the members of the crew so you had to pay a one third share. That could vary between sixteen shillings and a pound.

Lads of my age were not queuing up for these jobs. There were, however, plenty of seventeen year olds trying to get deferment from being conscripted by getting jobs afloat. Quite a lot of them managed to achieve this and a number remained at sea for the rest of their careers.

So when all the preliminaries were over; it just remained for me to convince my mother that I was going to sea. Mother had already said she would not hear of the idea, but to me it was not just an idea, it was my future.

She was worried about me being blown up at sea, as one of our next-door neighbour's sons had been. She had more or less got me a job as a boat builder's apprentice just because my hobby was woodwork. I had no intention of doing that if I had my way and so the arguments went on. Although my father was supportive of me, there seemed to be no way in which we could persuade my mother.

Going down to the docks whenever I had free time, I soon learned that there was a very good choice of select berths. After some thought, I applied for and was accepted as third hand in R. & W. Paul's sailing barge *Jock*. They had quite a fleet at that time. The *Jock* was said to be the best of the bunch, with a very sound hull and good gear. Of particular interest was that the company supplied coal for the cabin stove and the fo'c'sle cooking range, which was unheard of in most companies.

Then it was a question of nipping home and explaining that I had obtained this berth. Father was pleased for I was following in his footsteps. The Captain, 'Spero' Ling, was an old friend of his from the days when he had been a bargeman. However, mother was still unconvinced, and she ranted and raved, and said that there was no way I was going. Neither, she said, was she going to supply me with any blankets.

In those days you had to supply all the bedding that you needed yourself. Even with blankets you still had to pay about half a crown (12^1/$_2$p) for a very basic straw mattress. I think that I was always tired enough to sleep, whatever the bedding, after the day's work was over.

Finally the great day dawned, 29th December 1943. Overnight I had said that I was going, with or without their blessing. That ensured a good squabble and mum ended up by throwing some blankets down the stairs. Then I had the job of trying to cram them into my kit-bag along with everything else I thought I would need. I had made up the kit-bag myself, hand sewing the seams, whilst aboard the old *Quest* under the watchful eye of Skipper Hawkes. The bag had to be just so to pass his muster.

The Skipper had supplied me with a suit of oilskins and a good pair of long waders - a pair of Dunlop thigh boots - in the middle of the war. How, I did not know, what with rationing and coupons.

Finally I was ready to leave and the moment had arrived. I had said my goodbyes and then father had to hoist my kit-bag up on my shoulder for me. It was so heavy that I could never have got it there myself. The back garden, followed by a short length of passage had to be negotiated to get out. On reaching the road my shoulder was about ready to give way so down went the bag. I had just started to drag the bag along when a gentleman docker, yes there were still a few about in those days, old Steve Leeks, stopped to see if he could help.

His bike, being a typical docker's trade cycle, soon had my bag in its front box. He then pedalled away, promising to deliver my bag aboard the barge, which was lying at the Old Custom House berth along the north side of the Ipswich dock. Sure enough, by the time I got there Steve had put my bag on board. For some reason there was always a bond of friendship between us two. In later years I used to come to the dock in larger ships as Master. If Steve was in the gang to load or discharge, you could be sure there was always some reminiscing and the odd pint of wallop.

The first day or two aboard were spent being very busy polishing the brass work. The previous third hand had left some three weeks before, and the verdigris had started to take over. I was kept on my toes and Mick, the mate saw to it that I was never likely to be slack or get bored. At that time the fo'c'sle and the Master's cabin aft hadn't had their usual scrub outs. It was usual that every other day the Master's cabin, and twice a week the fo'c'sle, were supposed to be scrubbed and cleaned. I had to catch up with the system, and at the end of each day I was exhausted.

Mick Smith, the mate, was then in his mid-thirties. He had no intentions of going as Master himself but had the gift of teaching and I was a very willing pupil. From him and 'Spero' the Captain, I was certain to get an excellent grounding in every aspect of seamanship.

At last our turn came around for loading. As we were lying at the Custom House we had to get ourselves across the dock and down to the public warehouse on the south-west quay where we were going to load a cargo of potatoes. Third hands were called 'Joe' and as 'Joe' I had to scull across the dock with our dolly[1] rope, make it fast over there, and scull back to lend a hand to heave the barge across the dock. The type of craft that we were on did not have a dolly winch like some smaller craft. Our dolly rope had therefore to be taken back to the mastcase winch and hove from there. This made it at least a two-man job. One did the heaving and the other the pulling back on the rope, taking care to avoid riding turns. These would have fouled everything up, and there really would have been some lost tempers.

When we eventually reached the other side of the dock we had to run the rope out again from bollard to bollard until you came to the one at your berth. Then it was time to moor up and, if you were lucky, to have a cuppa. As the pace was a lot slower in those times you would usually get in the berth one day ready for the next day's work.

First thing in the morning we uncovered our main and fore hatches, slackened the sprit right off and held it clear of the main hatch by setting up the off-side rolling vang[2]. Then we went to the shore-side and let go the running and standing back stays[3], all this so that the crane was able to work unimpeded. The old steam cranes on that quay could certainly move, and the dockers, being paid on tonnage, made sure that they were kept going. In Ipswich docks at the time, dockers did a first-class job seldom, if ever, equalled in any other port I visited.

Having finally got our cargo on board we had to batten everything down and lash anything that could move. The mate and I then went to town with the deck scrubbers. With our loaded freeboard leaving the water within easy reach of our brooms, we were soon well washed down, the muck going over the side leaving the old girl shining like a new pin.

Captain 'Spero' Ling had his various calls to make. As he used to 'grub' the ship he had to like shopping. He also had to have his pint. At last 'Spero' said the tug was ordered and old Ted and his motor boat came to us. We were soon underway and, as the river was level with the dock at the lock gates, we were pulled straight through.

---

[1] The 'Dolly' was the small diameter winch barrel, above the anchor windlass, which carried a long rope or light wire used for warping the barge around docks and quays. [2] Vang, pronounced 'wang' - a wire to control the sprit end. The rolling vangs rigged when required to provide additional control in poor weather. [3] Stays - wires to support the barge's spars.

R. & W. Paul's *Jock,* laden in a crowded anchorage, aboard which Ivan started out as third hand.

It was only then that I began feeling a little apprehensive at seeing the dock receding astern with the thought that this was to be my first night at sea. It might have made a difference if there had not been a war on. I had never been outside the River Orwell but knew that German mines were scattered about outside the harbour and in the Swin channels, and also that there were still air attacks. I had every reason to be uneasy and think twice. But now I was committed and I had just to get on with it and hope for the best.

Although we were due to leave, we had a rather long and imposed stay at the Shotley Stoneheaps anchorage. The naval patrol kept saying that the inshore route had not been swept as the minesweepers were busy further out. Daily shouts across the water to the other waiting craft had the Captains deciding that this or that particular day was not the one. We stayed day after day owing mainly to the inclement weather, but sometimes Jerry had upset them with his mines. I was quite happy at this time as I had begun to settle. I was also able to take myself ashore on the mud and dig a few worms. The whiting were about so I was able to go back aboard and catch a few.

Those whiting increased our larder. After they were gutted we used to hang them up in the rigging to dry and let the wind do the rest. They were really smashing to eat and as there were no fridges in barges at sea we were lucky to have fresh food like that. Old 'Spero's 'salt pot' wasn't anything to shout about, but it was better than the food a lot of other people were getting to eat at the time. I think that 'Spero' used to come back from the pub via the vegetable fields because after he went for a beer, usually his bag came back with something in it. The larder was usually more than well stocked. Often we had to take the hatches off to vent the hold. At least we made that our excuse so we could nick a few spuds. Some of the other barges were loaded with brown raw sugar and we were able to do a swap. We always had sweet tea and the living was good for us. One or two had flour cargoes but they never seemed to get many bags broken. We were lucky if we got hold of more than a biscuit tin full. Still, that made a couple of 'duffs'. I reckon that if we had been rumbled at that time we would all have been shot at dawn!

At long last our departure day came, or at least at about five in the morning 'Spero' gave us a call. That was so that we could down a couple of mugs of tea and at the very first light in the sky respond to the order to heave short. Those two small words are very short but in the barging world mean a hell of a lot. First the riding light comes down and is put safely away. Then you start to heave the anchor chain in. As you heave it up it rides across the windlass[1] until there is no room for it to go further and you hook the dogs on the chain. This allows you to slacken the chain on the windlass barrel without loosing what you have just wound in. The chain can then be 'flet over' and away you go on the next heave and fleet until the Captain says, 'Short enough.'

---

[1] Winch principally used to retrieve anchor.

Whilst that had been going on, the chain had to be scrubbed clean of any mud that it may have picked up. On that occasion it was no problem as there was plenty of water around us.

The Captain went aft and made sure the kicking strap, which had stopped the rudder slamming about whilst we were at anchor, was slacked right off so we could steer. The mate and I worked like hell, for the order was given to set the topsail and prepare the foresail. Still jumping about, the mainsail was hooked into the main horse traveller, and slowly the main brails, lowers and middles were slacked away until the mainsail was full and smartly set.

'Spero' had the foresail pulled over to the starboard side and made fast. That meant that as the sail filled, it pushed us away to port. After it was let draw, we would have been paying away on the starboard tack. First though, before the foresail was let draw, it was allowed to fill and drive the head of the vessel round and that in turn broke the anchor away from its hold. The Mate and I then had to wind fast and furiously on the windlass to get the anchor hard up, and then cat[1] it.

As soon as we had done this it was time for tea again. Whilst I was making the brew, the mate was busy getting the bowsprit ready for lowering. The tea was hardly down our throats before Mick and I started lowering the bowsprit down. As soon as it was in position, the bobstay[2] was set up around the windlass barrel and hove down taut. The shrouds[3] were then set up tight and Mick had to set up the jib stay. As the weather was quiet, he let me go out along the bowsprit for the first time in my life, to release the jib from its gaskets. When I got back on deck we set the jib and I was proud of my effort!

Not so long after we had got things tidied up 'Spero' said to Mick that he would have the staysail set over the jib. Away we went for'ard again with Mick mumbling under his breath about the extra work the bugger was giving us. I had never seen a barge with all that canvas set before and I made certain that I made a mental note of how it was done. Mick had to take the short topmast stay out to the end of the bowsprit along with the staysail. It was no mean feat but soon it was there, and the staysail was out and set over the top of the jib. What a sight she must've been.

Doing all this work might have seemed to have taken half the day, but no, it was still only very early morning. We were under full sail and bowling along when came the order, 'Joe, get the kettle on!'

I had got things moving down below when 'Spero' came down to give me a hand to get the breakfast ready. I don't think that I have ever felt so hungry as I did that morning, but I was told to go back on deck and stand by with the mate while the Captain had his breakfast. Then it was Mick and I together. I had a real tuck in to bacon and eggs, fried bread and plenty of bread and marmalade and tea to finish. Rationing didn't seem to be in force that morning and I came away from the table well full.

---

[1] Hauling the anchor to one side well clear of the water, and lashing it to avoid damage to the hull and stem as the barge sails through the water. [2] A chain which keeps the bowsprit end from lifting when sails are set on the spar. [3] Shrouds - the main standing wires which support the mainmast, mizzen mast and bowsprit.

I got the washing up out of the way and then trimmed the wicks of the cabin oil lamps. Mick had told me that I might just be in with a chance to have a steer if the weather was good. I did plenty of flying about to complete my jobs, and was then told that I could take the wheel - it was magic for me. Under the guidance of 'Spero' and Mick I think I soon learned the art, and after that when the days were good I did plenty of steering. I knew that Mick was not keen on doing it so I got quite a lot of his share.

As the day progressed the wind had settled at about force five, and so it remained. 'Spero' had said that with a bit of luck, and if it kept up, we would be off Whitstable before dark. He hoped that we would be able to get in the harbour and so it turned out. After we had got over towards the Red Sand towers, we had stowed the staysail and the bowsprit jib, and hove the bowsprit back up to its harbour position. As I stood at the wheel doing my first trick whilst running before the wind, old 'Spero' was trying to tell me as much as he knew about Whitstable. Whelks and mud would be an apt description.

After our lying about for three weeks we had been able to get from Harwich to Whitstable in just a few hours and without any problems. The local 'huffler', mud pilot, or whatever you liked to call him, came aboard. We had a few hair-raising moments as we went round the pier end because quite a sea

The north Kent harbour of Whitstable, which dries out at low water.

was breaking. I didn't know until then that the mud inside the harbour was the only brake that anyone needed in this place. We ground to a halt about midway into the harbour and my first passage was over. Looking back, and as 'Spero' had commented at the time, and he was right.

Once we had moored we tidied up, making sure that everything was where it should be and that we had a stow that we from north of the estuary could be proud of. That first night I was too tired even to think of going ashore. I just curled up with a good book until I dropped off to sleep.

With our good passage behind us, the next day dawned with very inclement weather. It was blowing a full gale with very heavy rain so we did not have to worry about stripping the covers or taking the hatches off. It was a no-go day as far as unloading went, so we were left to our own devices. I had to scrub out the accommodation and clean the brass work before I was able to creep ashore for my first look around the place. I must say that at my age Whitstable did nothing to impress me and as my finances were really non-existent it was back to my books.

The bad weather continued, except that after a couple of days the rain turned to snow. We kept good fires going in the barge's cabin and fo'c'sle. These couldn't be beaten in cold snaps for warmth and snugness. About the fourth day the weather cleared and we were able to strip the covers and take the hatches off. All was not well, however, as after about a dozen sets had been taken out of the main hold it was decided that our cargo was rotten. It was found that when the bags containing the potatoes were stacked on the lorry they fell apart and the spuds fell out. We put the cover back on the hold and had to wait for the man from the Ministry to come and pass judgement.

We waited for three days, as did the other craft that had arrived with us, so the card schools were soon started. We didn't really mind lying there the way the weather was at this time. The Skipper found the beer good and his old cronies were there. We did manage to go to the pictures on one occasion so I suppose that a good time was had by all. As soon as the little man from the Ministry arrived the hatches had to be whipped off. He very soon passed judgement and said the top seven tiers would go for human consumption and the rest could go for cattle. Even those he had passed as fit for humans we knew would taste vile as our cooking pot had already told us!

After the last of our decaying cargo had been discharged, Mick and I had the job of trying to get the hold in some sort of order, and some job it proved to be. The rotten smell was everywhere and there seemed to be a squelchy layer under foot. We were both relieved after we had given it the first sweep and disposed of the bits of rotten potato. Only then did it begin to smell like a barge's hold again.

The skipper had by that time returned and told us that we had orders to go to London light1[1]. When I asked what part, so that I could drop a card home, he just said Albion Wharf, and that was it. We didn't know our next destination or even what the cargo would be. Cargoes were going to and from all sorts of different places in wartime, according to 'Spero'. The wharf was one of the company's so really the cargo was expected to be grain or malt.

Leaving the little harbour of Whitstable we were soon creeping along the Cant edge. As the winds were rather fickle it was a long time before we could really say that Whitstable was far astern. We were slowly dribbling along and as soon as it was high water it was time to bring up[2]. We had to obey the wartime no night-sailing rule and lay till the next day.

We didn't have a very quiet night as the wind had freshened and gone round back from the south to east- south-east. We tumbled about all night long and I think we were all glad to see the light of day come in, and for 'Spero' to say those couple of words, 'Heave short!' Soon we were underway again and with the wind holding from east-south-east we were going really well.

We had to pass through the boom defence vessels' gateway, just above the Chapman Head light. The wind died on us. The thing we had to do then was to avoid drifting into other barges which were also airing about quite close to us. Just before we had cleared the boom defence vessel and were about to enter the Thames I saw a sight that I would never forget.

There was this small tanker that had only just passed us and must have hit a mine. The ship disintegrated, for she was there one minute and gone the next. Although plenty of small craft rushed out and around the debris, 'Spero' didn't rate the chances at all for any survivors. And so my introduction to the Thames was far from being a happy one.

Soon we were passing a few of the older sailing barges that had been taken over by the Government. They sat in the river like dead ducks with a balloon sticking out of their heads. Some were manned with observers to try and spot the mines that the Jerries were dropping in the Thames at night. They

[1] Without any cargo. [2] To anchor.

had a very lonely life just being in the same place day after day. Others flew tethered barrage balloons to stop low flying German bombers.

At long last we made it to the top of Sea Reach and anchored in the Lower Hope. Very little time was wasted before we went below to stoke the fire up and soon we were warm and snug again, even if it was just for a few hours. Mick told me that had it been in normal times we would have been under way on the very last of the ebb on the late night tide. Being wartime we were able to have a good night's sleep.

It didn't seem very long before the relentless 'Spero' was shouting out again to let us know that it was time for us to be up and about. I will say that the old fellow always did make the first pot of tea of the day and it was the most welcome one at that. I had also at that time been getting used to my early morning fag, much against the wishes of the mate who did not like the smoke. 'Spero' used to smoke like a chimney and he taught me that if you saved all the fag ends, the thirty that I could afford would then make forty. When you were windbound for days on end even cold dry tea leaves were mixed with tobacco to eke out our smokes.

We were all too soon heaving up the anchor again and making our way up river. And what an eye-opener it proved to be for me, having been used to the River Orwell in all its glory and niceties. The Thames proved to be a river of bad smells most of the time. I thought that the heavy ware-housing of the river and the constant comings and goings of the tugs, lighters and shipping all spoilt the beauty that the river held. It was not long, however, before I realised the importance of the river to the nation itself at that time. The number of cargoes were many and varied and the Liberty ships from the U.S.A. were just tremendous in their contribution towards our war effort.

Eventually we reached Albion Wharf, just above the South Woolwich ferry. We had to do some very intricate manoeuvring down inside the lighter roads, but old 'Spero' didn't seem to worry. I stood there thinking he'll soon have to take the sail off her, but what I didn't know was that the tide set was very strong there and suddenly we touched the bottom and stopped. We stowed the gear and took a couple of lines away to the quay, slowly pulling ourselves alongside as the tide made. Even before we had finally moored up, the people on the quay were shouting at us to get the hatches off.

The chute was swung over the hold and we commenced to load maize. It went in very quickly and in about three hours we were loaded to our marks. As the tide had by that time finished flowing, 'Spero' decided that we would lie that tide and go as soon as we floated on the next. He wasn't at all happy after he had learned our destination for discharge, for he came aboard and told us the news that our trip was above the bridges, with all the extra work that entailed, to Battersea, at that time an area frequently hit by the German flying bombs.

We came off the quay in the early hours of the morning and dropped over to the lighter roads. There we were to lie and await the young flood tide and also the daylight. 'Spero' was not going to let us lie idle, for as soon as the light was in the sky we were about. There was a lot of hard work to do to get the gear ready for lowering down so that we could pass under the numerous bridges on the way to Battersea. Despite the extra work and risk I was really looking forward to this new experience.

The tug was supposed to pick us up in the lower pool, just below Tower Bridge. As the young flood made up we cast off only to be more or less becalmed shortly after. We were all a bit fed up as even on this short run the *Jock* only just managed to get to the lower pool on that tide.

The real work then began, for although we had been able to do some preparation we now had to get the bowsprit back inboard, drop the topmast, and finally lower the lot down to the level of the mast prop. Ours was about five feet from the deck. As soon as everything was down to this level, it all had to be lashed against any movement from passing traffic. The tugs and the 'up through' colliers (flat-irons) had a lot of way on as they came through these bridges, and so a fair amount of wash was created. Our lashing had to be very thorough!

Around noon the next day, the tug was alongside and nicely swung us round. We were soon passing under Tower Bridge and, after what seemed a very short tow, the tug was swinging us round head to tide again and placing us right on to our berth. After mooring up, we then had the job of heaving the gear up to clear the hatchways and make ready for discharge.

The suction hoses were soon into our fore and main holds, and a day and a half later the last of the maize went up the spout. We covered up and lowered the mast and gear ready for the tow down river. We were not at all happy as we learned that the owners had laid on for us to do two more of those trips! That meant a lot of work for us as we had to tow down to the Lower Pool and re-rig, sail to South Woolwich and load, sail back to the Lower Pool, unrig and tow up again for discharge, and then repeat it all over again.

It was whilst we were up there for our second trip that Jerry decided to intervene. It was about 1.30 in the morning and Mick and I had both been turned in for some time when 'Spero' called us and told us that the air raid siren had sounded and that he was going to the works air raid shelter. Mick and I decided to stay aboard.

As we were having a mug of tea all hell seemed to break loose. It turned out that a doodlebug[1] had struck part of the warehouse at the front. Two of the warehouse staff and 'Spero' were in the shelter by that time and its entrance had been blocked by debris. They had to be dug out of the rear escape hatch. As we all dug through and they finally came out, 'Spero' said he would never go into a shelter again.

---

[1] Nickname for the German V.1. rocket powered flying bomb.

We benefited in an unexpected way as our last trip was cancelled because of the damage to the warehouse, and we were all well pleased. After we had been able to sort ourselves out it seemed that the old *Jock* had not come to any harm. It was with some relief that we towed down and rigged out ready to go to sea.

We went to the North Woolwich buoys to wait a few days for orders. These buoys were known to the share bargemen as the starvation buoys, for whilst they lay here they received no pay. We were weekly paid so we didn't have to worry so much. However, boredom soon set in.

The few days turned out to be just under a fortnight. We finally received orders to go to Bellamy's Wharf to load a cargo of fishmeal for Ipswich. From the buoys to Bellamy's was just a short sail and that was done without trouble, up river on the flood tide and with just a nice commanding breeze, to me a very pleasant sail.

The tides were always busy with shipping and I soon got to know the hoots of the tugs and the ships blowing signals as they went to go astern or to turn round. It was seeing all this hive of activity that, I think, helped me make up my mind to try and stick to the coastwise and short-sea trade if and when the time came to go into power..

We arrived at the wharf and got ready to receive our cargo having had to wait until it was our turn to load. Then for the first time the shock of being told that the mate and I were expected to assist in the stowage of the cargo. What a stinking job that turned out to be as Mick and I had to stow the bagged fishmeal under the side decks, in the aft cupboard and beneath the mastdeck. After we had done for the day it became a battle to try and get ourselves and our clothes clean, as the smell of fishmeal had got right into everything. Mick used to just laugh and said it would take months to be free of it. At the time I believed him. He said that in all probability we would turn around and load another such cargo, and then would come his saying, 'Not to worry Joe!'

We lashed down and soon we were ready for sea. The next daylight high water had arrived, so it was time for us to make our departure. I know that I was glad to leave, and I'm sure the Skipper and mate both were as well, as the old Jerries were forever popping their doodlebugs over. We really didn't know how to take these, but we knew that as long as the engine kept going we were fairly safe[1].

The sails were set and filling; it was a welcome relief as the old *Jock* gathered way. She seemed to be in a great haste herself as she cleared the lighter roads. By that time I had been away from home for about five weeks and was very much looking forward to seeing my folks again.

The drill down river was as much as we could call normal, making a good fetch here and there, down leeboard and then up leeboard as we had to make the occasional board. All too soon it was low water and we were just off Grays, which the Skipper decided would be our berth for the night.

[1] The range of the flying bombs was dependent on fuel load. When the rocket motor ran out of fuel, the bomb would fall to earth.

After tea I decided to have an early night as the tide runs fairly hard along this shore. 'Spero' said this was his reason for not going ashore, but Mick reckoned the cash flow wasn't too good. As we had experienced a lot of lying about latterly I was inclined to agree with the Mate.

I had looked forward to my early night, and got nicely settled down with my book, but I was soon over and away to sleep. However, the old Luftwaffe had different ideas, and they were soon dropping their incendiary bombs all around us. That's when 'Spero' came to call us out saying that we would drudge round the bight to Gravesend. Although we were not supposed to be underway at night nobody challenged us. We set no sails at all, just tripped the anchor and let the tide do the work. It set us around the corner and away down through Gravesend Reach. Passing the Tilbury landing stage we could see the fire crews were very busy everywhere we looked. Once we had cleared below Tilbury we seemed to have left the danger zone, and thankfully so. We were soon down to the Denton anchorage, just below the Ship and Lobster, Palmer's pub as it was known to us lads. It was there that quite a lot of us tasted our first real pints. The landlord and landlady really took to all us youngsters whilst we would wait there for our Skippers, and they would always see to it that we had a drink of some sort and the odd pie.

Next day, 'Spero' decided that the weather was not fit for us to go on, and decided to go and use the telephone to let the owners know where we were. That meant me putting him and the mate ashore and being back at the allotted time to fetch them.

The greengrocer, the baker and all the rest of the tradesmen, used to call at the pub, so one was able to buy most things as well as beer. When it was time for us lads to fetch our Skippers back, we would always be early so that we were able to see the very congenial host, Mr Jim Palmer and his good lady, who was like a second mother to us. She would never see anyone go without something, even if they were broke.

On one occasion when I had gone ashore to pick up the Skipper and mate from there, the Skipper had been shopping for the galley and was carrying a kit-bag with bread in it. He had also been very busy sampling the beer and clearly had imbibed enough because he bought me a 'small brown', an otherwise unheard of generosity!. On returning to our boat at the jetty he went to throw the kit-bag into the boat, but missed completely and it ended up in the river. 'Spero', without hesitation threw himself in after the kit-bag and, for a man who could not swim a stroke it was a very foolhardy thing to do. Mick the mate pulled him out and we had to get him back aboard as soon as we could. Mick pushed him below to warm through, and within a couple of hours he seemed to have made a total recovery.

Unlike his swim at the Ship & Lobster, not all the Skipper's problems were of his own making. Later we were sailing over the Spitway just off

Clacton. Whilst the mate and I were below eating the last of the duff, the German and British planes were having a dogfight above us. A piece of shrapnel hit our mizzen mast, just missing 'Spero' who was at the wheel. He took a dive head first down into the cabin and gave his nose a real whack, which became known as his 'shrapnel wound'!

Once clear of the Spitway the wind stayed very favourable for us and we had a nice leisurely sail home. That first homecoming was a bit of a surprise. As I walked indoors with my bag of dirty washing on my shoulder, Mother said, 'Well what do you think now?' And I said it was great.

But that's where I told a big lie. If I had told the truth, and looking at my hands raw from chilblains, I would have to have admitted that it was a very basic and hard existence and packed it up there and then. I should have taken the boat-building apprenticeship that I had been offered. But remembering the aggravation that I had when I wanted a couple of blankets to go away with, I thought I had better remain silent.

We probably spent a few days windbound on most trips, but as we were weekly paid servants, it didn't make a lot of difference to us. When wind and weather were against us we didn't get underway until it suited the Skipper. Many of those on other barges worked by the share, receiving a proportion of the earnings of the vessel. They had to do a lot more than us to get along. When I spoke to Mick about it, he said never sail by the share. Unfortunately, I could see that I would not be able to take his advice if I was to reach my goal. The third hand's wages were not enough to live on, and the move to mate had to be made as soon as possible after having learnt enough of the mate's duties.

For the next eight months I sailed as third hand on the *Jock* and I found my shipmates great to get along with. They gave me the foundation of my career and taught me what good seamanship really meant.

Chapter IV
AN IRON COFFIN

I learned of a mate's berth on a barge lying on the other side of the dock, waiting to load her cargo. Old 'Spero' had given me plenty of sound advice which I had chosen to ignore. I had by that time become quite handy and just assumed that he was doing his best to keep me so that they didn't have to teach another third hand, having brought me to a useful standard.

If, after about three months, any third hand had not begun to get it together, he soon found himself back on the beach and another lad would take the berth. The Skippers didn't like this idea as they had to start the training all over again. Once you were trained in their ways they wanted you to stop with them, but I chose to go.

I contacted the *Cambria's* Skipper after the pub had got rid of him. Although I had difficulty in understanding his slurred speech, I understood that the job was mine if I wanted it, and I grabbed it. I thought that I was among the great clan, a barge mate of a coaster at the age of just fourteen and a half. The Skipper told me some, but not all, of my conditions of employment to my cost as I was to find out later.

Cambria was an old 'Ironpot', commonly known as an iron coffin. Barges, such as her, were built at Southampton to a standard design and carried 150 tons of cargo to sea. The hold space was tremendous, 150 tons carried with a freeboard of less than six inches. They were always wet if there was more than a ripple on the water. These barges had a light rig handled very easily by the man and boy, often referred to when people speak of barge crews. There were times, of course, when we could have done with a lot more.

The *Cambria* was a share barge, each crew member receiving a share of the operating profits. This meant that if there were no cargoes, and therefore no work, there was no pay. One could, however, leave without so much as a goodbye at any time as the Skipper had no legal hold over you once the hold was empty at any port. Often we were broke and with nothing to come. That's when you tightened your belt, whilst you waited for the next cargo. You couldn't have a sub until you had orders.

Cargoes at that time were fairly plentiful. There was sugar to London, cargoes of malt and timber from Ipswich to Maldon and Heybridge Basin, and cargoes going outwards to all places from London.

I soon learned that we were low in the water whenever loaded and continually wet through. We had to be extremely well battened down and

The 'Ironpot' *Cambria*, seen on the ground and showing the rounded chine, typical of her type.

lashed very thoroughly for just a short trip in good weather, otherwise there was a real chance of an unplanned trip down to see Davy Jones.

Our method for lashing was with wires going along each side of the hatches on a loop system from rings along the coamings and then being picked up in the middle of the hatch. By using handy billy[1] tackles the wires were pulled tight. The ropes were coiled in a rectangular shape and then lashed very securely in the four corners. Those hatchways were continually awash when you were loaded and the lashing had to be the very best that you could do.

One advantage of the *Cambria* was the very large hold that she had for a craft of her size. It was the one good thing, as there was not really any trimming of cargoes to be done except for timber or coke.

Creature comforts were non-existent in those craft. The cabin had very little in the way of timber trim so the berths were always wet with condensation and freezing cold. I would think that a few winters in one of these craft might have been a killer. However, some of my friends had many a winter in them, as they worked from their home port of Grays by the Thames, where E. J. & W. Goldsmith, the owners, had their repair yard.

We were about to load a cargo of sugar and I was landed with the task of sweeping the hold clean. The accommodation had not had a scrub out either. As *Cambria* only carried two crew, it fell to the mate to do all the chores, whilst the Skipper was in the pub, usually for as long as his money lasted out.

With all that work in front of me I just had to get on with it. Three times I had gone over that hold just to make sure that it was good enough to take on the cargo. The Ministry Inspector was a bit of a stickler and insisted that the hold was spotless before he would let you load. The cargo that we were about to take was bagged raw sugar from the local beet factory at Sproughton, just outside Ipswich. It came aboard the barge from railway trucks, with dockers doing the handling. We, the crew, had just to help a docker turn the bag, each of which weighed twenty-two stones, off his back. It was no mean feat for a man to keep that up all day. At the day's end, I was shattered like the docker. The Skipper wasn't, for he managed to be stuck in some pub somewhere ashore, or sharing a bed as he liked to put it.

We loaded the cargo without any stack above deck at all. A stack would have been a pain to lash and a job to sail with, as some of the less spacious craft had to do in order to get their tonnage. I was very thankful that we did not need one.

After the cargo had been loaded the Skipper had been able to collect a good sub from the brokers. For the next few days, whilst a fair wind was blowing, the Skipper was ashore supping up the ale and chasing the ladies. We were lying in the lay-by berth and whilst other craft were going away we were still in the dock. No matter what I said, the Skipper didn't take any notice of me. At that time in my career I was so keen to be getting on with the job so I was very despondent about lying in the dock missing the favourable

---

[1] A general purpose tackle.

slant south. However, the Skipper hadn't any intention of sailing until he was nearly skint. At last it was time for us to go and so the motor boat came and towed us away from our berth and we were let go at the end of Cliff Quay and were on our own.

I was soon to find out that I was very much on my own, receiving little help from the Skipper in setting the sails, and then only when he really had to do something. As there was quite a strong north by north-west breeze we didn't have to set too much canvas, only the topsail, foresail and about half the mainsail.

We anchored down at Fagbury, where we were to lie for the next two days, and that's when I discovered the Skipper's sea stock was just a pot of jam and a loaf of bread. I was given to understand that the ladies had had the extra rations from the Skipper's ration book.

In the *Cambria* we both grubbed ourselves, and seeing how he was living I decided to let the system remain. Being there for a couple of days wasn't very pleasant. The Skipper hardly spoke and the fish didn't really come on the feed, so when he said, 'Right, let's away!' I was soon jumping about getting us under way.

With a nice sailing breeze from the nor'ard it was very much like a pleasure sail, except for the grumbles from behind the wheel. That turned out to be his usual way, so after a short time I didn't take any notice of him. At the end of the day we had just got to the Blacktail Spit and it became very dark. We went on to the Shoeburyness boom and brought up. As the boom had closed for the night we had to sit there for about ten hours or so. The fishing along here was great at all times so the rigging had plenty of fish hanging there next morning soon after we had got under way.

Another day or so was spent trying to get to Silvertown as the wind turned fickle and was very variable at times. On arrival we were behind no less than eighteen other craft, and taking our turn we were nearly on a starvation diet before we started to unload the cargo.

We didn't receive the full freight money until all the cargo was out. The Skipper didn't appear until he was nearly destitute. If you had a couple of quid to come, that was when he used to bring it to you, and probably try and borrow one back at the same time.

At any rate, we finally got rid of the remainder of the sugar and I had the grand total of £6 for my first trip on mate's share. Then it was down to the old 'starvation buoys' at North Woolwich. It was only a short hop and we were soon moored up awaiting orders and the Skipper was away home again for nearly a week.

At last we received orders, if you could call them that, for we had to go to Beckton gas works to load a cargo of coke for the Isle of Sheppey, to Sheerness dockyard as it turned out. My share of that was to be about £2. 10s. 0d. (£2.50). It would just about buy my rations for the week and not a lot more for the 'lay days'. At any rate it would keep the wolf from the door.

The 'Starvation Buoys' at Woolwich where barges would lie awaiting orders.

As that was the first time that I had loaded a cargo of coke it seemed as if I had a lot to learn. The hold was soon full to the top of the coamings. We then stood the hatches inside the bulwarks, lashing them through the handles. The coke was allowed to fill right to the top of these and then it was heaped another couple of feet higher in the middle.

We had to reef the skirt of the mainsail to clear the stack and then we were ready for the off. Soon we were away down the river, bringing up once again at Grays for the Skipper's gadabout. It wasn't long before he was broke and we were away again, this time to complete the trip without any more distractions. Apart from some problems getting into the dockyard on our arrival we had a perfect trip.

As soon as we had berthed, the crane was into the hold and rushing the coke out. Within the space of seven and a half hours the cargo was on the quayside and we could have been ready to take on another. However, we were not so lucky, and had to get out and go and lay up off Queenborough. That gave the Skipper the chance for a few more nights at home.

One morning, just a week later, the Skipper was on the quayside yelling for me to go and pick him up. As soon as he got into the boat he started moaning because our orders were to go to the Surrey commercial docks to load a cargo of timber to go to Maldon for discharge.

It appeared he didn't like the place of loading, the cargo, or the discharge port. Unlike the Skipper, I looked forward in great anticipation to that coming trip for it was all completely new to me, both the ports and cargo.

The passage up river passed very well after we had cleared Sheerness and got through the Swatchway. From somewhere fortune smiled on us and we picked up a cracking breeze; it came up about east-south-east and so we made rapid progress up the Thames right to the lock head of the Surrey dock. I think it took nearly as long to get into the dock as it did to sail up, but finally we made it. We then had a steady heave up the dock to our ship to wait our turn to load.

In my previous berth aboard *Jock* we hadn't loaded timber so again I had quite a lot to learn. Just sorting out the lashings seemed quite a job, with the Skipper telling me how everything had to be. That's when he told me our cargo was going to be tree trunks. As the old *Cambria* was a share barge, we would take almost any freight going, and to anywhere, as long as the Skipper knew how to get there.

To load the tree trunks, everything in the hold had to be let go so the trees could be lowered in. That included the heavy chains that went across our hold to help keep the barge's shape. As soon as the cargo was to the level of these chains they had to be fastened again. Loading was carried on over the top of them until the hold was completely full.

It was necessary to completely cover up and batten down the hatches, before pieces of timber were laid across the hatchway and loading continued. That meant that you started from the bulwark line going right across the hatches to the other side. As you went back with the next tier, you loaded the timber between the previous two so that the new tier would work out one baulk less across and so on until the Skipper said, 'That's it!' and the finished height had been reached.

We had to leave the berth at the same time as we lashed down, and had our work cut out to cope with both tasks at once. As the timber was considered an import it meant that you only had three tides to be out of the dock or else you incurred extra dock charges. As this was a share barge each crew member had his share of these to pay, so perhaps the haste to get out could be understood.

We enjoyed a nice steady sail down the river and stopped at Grays for our stores, paraffin, etc., and also for the Skipper to have his sub from our yard and then another couple of days for his beer!

When we had at last got away I had hopes of a fast and good passage to make up for the lying about. Alas, it was not to be, and the best that we could do was to get down to Southend and hopefully to only lie for the night. Next morning all hell seemed to break loose for the wind had shot into the east-south-east and was blowing very strongly. The Skipper said we would try and get into Sheerness for shelter.

It was a very wet passage for a couple of hours and we were both very pleased when we had passed Garrison Point and found the peace inside. We were in a nice snug anchorage among a few others who were also waiting for a slant that would let us all go down the Swin.

After a couple of days the Skipper, who lived at Rainham, Kent, came back from home, had a couple of pints in the Old House at Home at the top of the causeway and declared that we were off, and so away we went.

The breeze had kindly gone right round to the south'ard for us so we had a lovely fair wind. Although it was very cold, we couldn't complain and after a great run we got down to the Whitaker beacon early. The wind then came out of the south-east and blew a lot harder. It was just the job for us and we were really getting along through the Spitways and up the Blackwater.

As the rain pelted down and the wind blew even more strongly we were able to sail right up to the wharf at Sadds, above Maldon town quay. This saved the costs of the motorboat towage that we would normally have had to pay to berth us. It also helped to convince me that I hadn't got too bad a Skipper. I could put up with his boozing as his sailing seemed very good to me at that time, inexperienced as I was.

I had discovered from talking with other Mates that my settlements were not all that they should have been. I was really being done down on the finances each trip, only by the odd couple of bob (10p), but enough to set the blood boiling. On those days the Skipper and I were always at loggerheads and that was when I decided to look for another berth. I had reached the stage where I could have thrown him over the side, assuming he hadn't thrown me over first. He then got around to talking me out of it, so we had a sort of truce and I thought I would give it a few more trips to see how it went.

Unloading the tree trunks took quite a long time as the pace at Maldon was a lot different from all the other places that I had been to until then. The old crane was panting and blowing with the weight of some of these logs. We had orders this time, even before we had unloaded, and the Skipper was raring to go. I am pretty sure the reason was that he was skint again. We finally got rid of the last of the cargo and were soon behind the motorboat and away.

After passing the end of the promenade we cast off our tow and were away on our own. We only had a short trip to make as we were bound to Alresford to load a cargo of grit. It turned out a twelve-hour jaunt, for by the time we had sailed down the Blackwater and into the River Colne, we had to bring up and wait until just before high water when the Skipper decided that we could go into the creek.

That was not a very good place to have to take a barge in the dark, through the railway bridge and alongside a wooden jetty, but it was done without any hesitation. We turned in as soon as we moored up and were ready to load at daylight next morning.

It was a very blustery sort of day, but the loading was quick and before very long we were battening down the hatches. As soon as she floated, we were off and away. The Skipper's bread and jam had to last him longer that trip for there were no shops at Alresford.

I knew he wanted money, so the barge had got to go. Blowing about force five, it didn't need much imagination to see that we were in for a very wet trip. The wind was from the south-east, so it meant a slog out to the Spitway and we were like a half-tide rock. The Master's kitty was long empty so she just had to go and go she did. All the time we were looking for the slant that never came, and to make matters worse the wind had gone further round to the southward and had increased to about force six. As we were over by the Whitaker Beacon it was a toss-up to see if we should go up the Whitaker or carry on. The Skipper was broke so we carried on. Once we were committed to going on, the Skipper had to think about the night's berth. We couldn't have lain safely or comfortably anywhere along the Essex Shoebury shore, so he decided that we would try and work over to the Kent side.

As the tide made and came in so did the swell. The broken water looked very angry. As the day went along, we had reduced sail dropping down the head of the topsail. The *Cambria* seemed to be going as fast as before and still very easy as far as the gear went, although very wet. Without warning the roping to the foresail sheet decided to give out. The Skipper said that I would have to do the repair, and what a job that turned out to be! No way could I, or anyone else, do much out there with the palm and needle. The only thing that could be thought up was to put a chain snotter[1] between the cringles to relieve the strain. That proved to be all right and held out until we were able to do a proper repair later.

We had to sail that much freer from the wind so our progress was slowed considerably and we lost ground. The time taken over the sail repair had also cost about an hour, so tempers were frayed again. At long last we had passed inside the Cant Edge buoy and had found a good sounding so the Skipper was able to bring us up to our anchor. As there were still a couple of hours to go to the high water it was not very comfortable to lie anywhere. As soon as the tide began to ebb, it soon smoothed off, allowing us to get some grub going and have a mug of tea which helped tempers to cool a little. The Skipper even said he was pleased that I had kept my cool when I had been under pressure and that was a good sign, so I was quite pleased with myself inwardly. I felt that praising the Skipper would have been in order, but then he might have thought that I had taken a better liking to him. There was no way that I could change my opinion with respect to his boozing and lazing about. His general outlook made us two opposites. Still I couldn't criticise his seamanship, so live and let live I said to myself, and still do.

[1] A loop in a small piece of rope or chain, or an iron ring.

That night passed very slowly for she was rolling and sheering about very badly. The Skipper spent quite a few moments during the night at the top of the cabin ladder making sure that we held on. I know we were very pleased to see the daylight roll in. As soon as it was light enough, we both had a go at the foresail sheet. Once we had done a bit more in the way of repairs, we got underway and were pleased when we passed inside the boom defence gateway. I think the Skipper said the very same words that I also felt, 'Thank God for that!' We jogged along up Sea Reach and as was often the case the wind seemed as if it was fining away quite a bit.

All too soon it was time to bring up again, and both of us were swearing about the time that we had had to waste on the foresail repairs. Still, that couldn't be helped, and we could only be thankful that we had been able to do the repair, for it could have turned into a lifeboat job, so the Skipper assured me. We turned in and were soon asleep, not having had much the previous night.

In the river the Skipper was a master at knowing every nook and cranny and I think he had already made up his mind on how to make up some of our lost time. As soon as it was low water, the bugger had me out and we were getting underway in the pitch dark and sailing up the river. I was on the wheel after we had been underway about an hour with strict instructions to keep a very sharp look out. Alas, very shortly afterwards I was in trouble. I think I must have been half asleep, but only a short time after looking under the lee of the mainsail we had come a cropper with the tripod of the Middle Blyth boom which got fouled up with the mainsail sheet.

The only thing that I could do was to yell for the Skipper. At the same time as I was yelling I let go of the mainsheet, and so the sheet was allowed to unreeve. The Skipper came flying up, shouting all kinds of obscenities and told me to go and brail the mainsail up. That was some problem with the sheet flying through the air. The lowers and middles had fallen out, so were of no use to me to help to get the foot of the mainsail under any sort of control. Still, we got there in the end and, as usual, we had then to put things right again.

To try and reeve the mainsheet in the pitch dark was no simple matter, although it didn't seem anything after it was done. The Skipper kept on with his pacing back and forth, especially as we had no right to be underway. He kept thinking the police would spot us and think we were in trouble and would come over and offer to help, when that was just what we didn't want. At any rate we were soon over to the west side of the Lower Hope. 'That's as far as we are going,' said the Skipper and again we brought up, but only a few miles further on. Still, 'That's barging' as they say and that's the sort of life the bargeman leads every day. It was a complete and unique way of life of their own, one very different to life on land, and one that I was beginning to accept as mine and was very proud to be part of.

It was 'Heave short!' again soon and I must say it was a pleasure! We had a really cracking sail and were able to make the run right up to the mouth of Bow Creek. As soon as we had got a turn on the lighter roads outside, one of the river toshers came to us with an offer to put us into our berth in the creek. It was agreed and the charge just came to as much sugar as we could let them have. We still had quite a bit left from our sweepings of raw sugar and the lads aboard the tug were very happy with what we were able to offer. They gave us some tea sweepings, no doubt from some lighter's hold, and that's how the world kept turning for some of us in those wartime days.

Once secured, the Skipper was off up the city to collect a sub. For a change he came back aboard the same day and gave me my princely earnings of just a fiver, so again I wasn't very pleased. To top it all we had the very worst of orders, back to Woolwich 'starvation buoys' with no more wages until we got orders to load a cargo, whenever that might be.

Once we were emptied we had a nice easy sail down to Woolwich. On the buoys I was glad to see quite a few of my old mates there. We had some good card schools. It also meant that any of us who had a few bob shared with those who didn't, for a run to the flicks, the odd pint, and of course not forgetting the fags. Sometimes there was a girl, picked up along the way.

Another full week was to pass on the buoys at Woolwich before the long awaited Skipper's shout came from the park railings. I was soon sculling my way over to the park bank. The Skipper told me we had orders to proceed to Charlton Buoys to load a cargo of hooves and horns[1] for discharge at Queenborough. Charlton is not very far from Woolwich, and we had good time to get up as it would be another couple of days before they would be ready to load us. The Skipper said we would go on the next day's flood. It seemed to me that we had no sooner got underway than it was time to stow up and get a turn alongside a lighter there. Then we had to run our ropes up aboard the ship, and report to the ship worker. His warehouse was the ship and he could tell from the ship's manifesto when your cargo would be likely to appear. He said that ours wouldn't show until late next day; home went the Skipper again and I was left to my pastimes.

I used to like having a good look around some of the ships when I had the chance. This was one of those times, as I was given a conducted tour by the Second Mate. I explained that I would probably be out of barges within a few years. I was therefore trying to gather all the information that I could to try and point myself in the right direction for the future. I had a very good look around, and was given a carton of fags. That was the first time that I had held a sextant in my life, and a right proud lad was I. The next day the ship's derricks were soon in action and even my Skipper was aboard quite early. Once we had got a start the cargo came aboard quickly. Along with the hooves and horns were the terrible smells and the biggest bloody maggots that I have ever seen, but there was worse to come.

[1] Hoof and horn was a 'by-product' of the many abattoirs. It was ground down for use in mainly industrial glues. There was a glue factory in Queenborough Creek.

Once the cargo was on board we had to just drop back clear of the berth so the next craft could go alongside. It was then a question of me getting the hatches on to cover up the holds while the Skipper had to go and sign for the cargo. As soon as he came back on board we set the canvas and, with a spring off from one of the other craft, we sheared away from the ship's side on the starboard tack paying away to the north and midstream.

Going down river we had no problems, with the *Cambria* going fine, just a little trim here and there to the sails, and a few ups and downs to the leeboards, but mostly reaching to a fair wind. In the Thames to Medway Swatchway the Skipper was doing his best with long and short tacks through the channel. As usual, we were letting the leeboards act as the lead line, just let the one down touch, and then go round on the other tack. But on one occasion, having just touched on the windward side, the old girl just kept going and then gave a shudder and stopped. We saw that we were there until the next tide flowed beneath and around us and gave us the lift to get going again.

At least during our short stay there the weather kept fine for us. Soon it was time for us to get underway again and after another pleasant little sail, we were lucky to have just enough water to get into Queenborough Creek. Inside the creek there was just black oozing mud flats. To stop we had shot the barge up on to the mud and that allowed us to give the sails a rough stow up. I then leapt into the barge boat to run our dolly wire ashore, get back on board as fast as I could and heave away on the dolly winch to get the barge moving into our discharging berth.

When all this was done the Skipper was soon washed and away ashore and off home, or to some other shore side harbour. Then it was my turn to wash and away ashore to the 'flicks', and on the way back buy fish and chips for supper. I thought I should be good for a few hours sleep, but it was not to be. It was very warm below decks for I had left a good fire when I went ashore and so there was plenty of condensation, but I soon got turned in with the old book out.

In a very short while I heard this sort of scraping sound coming from right above me on deck. Being the stupid youngster that I was, I didn't think that anything much could be up there. However, I turned out, and still a little weary climbed the cabin ladder to the deck. I then pulled the cabin hatch right back - we always used to leave the hatch about three inches open to let in a little air.

As I did so I could hear squeaking and on looking around I couldn't believe what I was seeing. I was looking at an army of large rats and they were going through the hooves and horns and anything else they could have a go at.

I dived back down below and pulled the hatch over, that time without three inches left for air. I lay there for the rest of the night, but sleep wouldn't come to me, for I had seen rats the likes of which I'd never seen before. I could only describe them as little donkeys! I wasn't afraid of them; I just didn't like them. When I was at school I used to go out to the slaughter houses with a gentleman known as Nobby, the Rat Catcher. His method of catching rats was to block off all the holes that we could find except three. One was for the powder pump to go in, one for the little Terrier dog Nigger to stand over and the other one used to be mine. I used to stand there, and as the rat put its head out, I used to kill it with an iron pin. For each one I got tuppence (1p) for its tail.

I decided that the types of cargo we were carrying were not for me and after that cargo was out, so was I.

Next day it poured with rain, so there was no work; only the vile smell of the cargo and the knowledge that the rats would be back that night once it was dark. The Skipper had rung up to check on the vessel's situation and the shore-side office had given him the information, and that was it as far as he was concerned. He never even asked if the mate was okay or not. Still, that was his way. At any rate, we got rid of the cargo the following day and then had to get out of the berth because another barge had arrived, and he was ready to get rid of his cargo.

As I had no Skipper there to take her out of the creek, the other barge Skipper told me to just slack the mainsail out to the sprit, cast the lot off and just let her blow across to the other side of the main fairway. I should let go the anchor

The 'Ironpot' *Cambria* turning to windward whilst empty, on her way to load a cargo.

near Deadman's Island[1] and, although nervous, I managed it. After a nice cup of tea, the old body steadied up a bit and I was able to take stock of my position.

First I decided that I would scrub the cabin out and leave the hold open for a day or so, so that it lost some of the stink. After a few hours like that the old girl became habitable again. It was then just a question of waiting for the return of the Skipper, with or without orders, for I was going to be off as soon as he was back.

After lying there for a couple of days, still on my own, the wind shot round to the south and was really freshening up, so I was getting a bit concerned. I gave her lots of chain and hoped that she would behave herself. It was during the third night that the old girl decided to have a look ashore - by that I mean that she decided to drag her anchor.

I was asleep in the cabin and heard nothing at all; the first I knew was when there was a bump followed by a crunch. Throwing on a pair of trousers I was quickly on deck and it was only then that I realised that it was thick with rain and a horribly black night. I saw that the poor old *Cambria's* rudder was rubbing under the quarter of one of the old wooden inshore minesweepers. Our rudder, being iron, was not doing the old sweeper any good whatsoever, and the Sub-Lieutenant on board her was not taking kindly to any of it. That was one time where Navy manpower came into full use. A rating took ropes from me, one leading from our main horse and another from our offside, which were both made fast to the sweeper. The Sub-Lieutenant then detailed the lads forward to heave our anchor up.

With the wind on our port side we were soon blown alongside the sweeper and I was able to clear the anchor which had a double turn around its stock. There was no way that the anchor would have held without first being cleared.

All that was done in the pitch dark and pouring rain and for no pay, as our hold was empty. The Navy lads had given me a couple of packets of fags, so I was soon off below for a good old 'puff up'. I thought I might get the rest of the night in my bunk, but about a couple of hours later the tug the Navy had sent along to get rid of me from alongside their sweeper arrived. I'll swear to anyone that the tug was bigger than the barge. I was promptly given a rope from the tug and told to let go from the sweeper. I managed this on my own without anymore ceremony than that, and I was hauled back over across to a good berth just off Deadman's Island. I let go the tug and the anchor, rigged the anchor light and was away down to my bunk. I could still feel the old girl roaring about so I jumped out of the bunk again and swiftly lowered the leeboards. After that the *Cambria* behaved herself for the rest of what had been a long and busy night.

I awoke early in the morning and the old fishing gear was soon over the side as I tried to catch a little something for the larder. And so it was for the next couple of days, reading and fishing, and not really enjoying either as the money was gone. Fortunately, due to the helpful Navy lads, I was still able to have a smoke.

[1] Supposedly named after its use as a disposal location for the bodies of victims of the plague.

Eventually the day arrived when the Master came back aboard and said 'I've got some money for you.', and I got the sum of two pounds and fourteen shillings (£2.70), that being the freight money. He then said that we still didn't have any orders and that he was off home again for a couple of days. I told him my bags were packed and that I was finished with the old *Cambria*. As the cabin had been scrubbed out and the hold and decks were clean I knew that I was at liberty to go.

There was then a little row but no tears, and as the Skipper knew that I would and could go, we both went ashore together. He bought me a beer but I left him in the pub as I started up the road on the long haul home.

I later realised that I had learnt a lot from this man, although I didn't always see eye to eye with him or appreciate his funny ways. But, he being the vessel's Master, he was in the right. I was at the sort of age, I suppose where I was arrogant and pompous and thought that I knew it all. But, with all that, he taught me a lot, and the training he gave me helped me no end in later life and for which even to this day I thank him.

44   After leaving the old *Cambria* I discovered that there was nothing more depressing, especially at my age, just about coming up to fifteen, than to leave a ship. I had a very large kit-bag and a handgrip and a very long passage to get home. There were few cars on the road at that time and it seemed unlikely that I was going to get a lift.

I was most surprised that I hadn't got far up the road before I was offered a lift as far as Ridham Dock, which I was very glad to accept. The lorry driver thought that I was crazy to be trying to get to Ipswich that way. When we arrived at Ridham Dock, I learned that they had a little railway that ran up to Sittingbourne. I was soon aboard a wagon and thought that I was really going places. After a very short run I realised that we were at Sittingbourne and was able to just pop round to the main station and board a fast train to London.

London was confusing. I was really lost and becoming very aware of the task that lay before me to try and find the strength to get myself and all my worldly goods across the city to Liverpool Street station. Somehow, at long last, I managed to get there, and collapsed in a heap. Before long, and without too much trouble, I was able to catch a train for Ipswich and home.

When I had arrived home and given Mum the dirty washing, I thought that I had better pop down to the docks and see what, if anything, was on offer. At R. & W. Paul's office I was offered a berth as mate on the barge *Lady Jean*, subject to the Master agreeing to accept me.

When I got down to the berth where the *Jean* was lying, I could not believe that I had even been considered, the barge's sheer size carried me away. After just a moment's hesitation I leapt aboard and was soon being quizzed by the Master. He was particularly interested as to what I had done since I had left the *Jock*. He told me that he thought the job would be much too heavy for me, and that it was also only a temporary berth until a mate came along who was over twenty-one years old, as that was an insurance requirement to allow the barge to operate to the full extent of her trading limits.

He said the berth could be mine if I wanted to give it a go. He then said that if there should be any trouble, any girls brought on board or anything like that, I could consider myself for the sack. I had to agree to this sermon, and he then said that I could start the job straight away.

I was very pleased to be a weekly paid servant again, receiving four pounds and five shillings (£4.25p) a week. My own father's wage at the time was the princely sum of three pounds, two and sixpence (£3.12$\frac{1}{2}$p), so I had landed a very good job. The only problem was that I had no way of knowing how long I was going to be in it.

The Master of the *Lady Jean* at that time was considered to be the Commodore of R. & W. Paul's fleet and Captain Frank Lucas was certainly a different man from my previous Skipper, never swearing at his crew or anybody else that I can remember. The man knew just what he wanted and went for it without hesitation, and was in my opinion a gentleman.

Once I had been given the berth, I was going to do my best to make very sure that I kept it. I didn't take long to realise that if I kept my eyes and ears open Frank would and could teach me a great deal which I could tuck away inside my head for the future.

I am very pleased to say that I did quite a few trips with Frank, each one having its own little amusements to take the boring times away. I came to appreciate the smooth way the Master conducted the running of the barge, and it was really great to be part of the crew. I say crew, because in the *Lady Jean* we carried a third hand, which meant that we could and did have better cooked food for there was always someone to look after its preparation and also to keep an eye on it whilst it was cooking. Provided that we had the raw materials, we lived quite well, especially when one considers that we were about halfway through the Second World War, with all its shortages.

We carried quite a lot of barley to London from Ipswich. During one trip we had a very near miss from the old German with his rocket. It was just as we were going through the King George Dock and passing through the swing bridge of the Royal Albert Dock that a V2 rocket landed close to the lock gates.

There was a great loss of life as the dock workers were caught going to lunch. The actual blast went a very long way, greatly damaging our sails, and lumps even went out of our topmast. At least we were able to heave a sigh of relief that we were all still in one piece, but I knew that day there were many who didn't make it. We were soon to know, once we reached the top of the Victoria Docks, that there had been casualties. There was no sign of the dockers aboard our ship. The only man we could trace was the 'Ship worker', for the lads had heard there had been a 'major one' on the pier head – their words! The dockers had therefore gone home out of respect to their colleagues who had been killed, and the whole dock was brought to a standstill.

By the morning a lay person would not have known anything had happened, as the dockers laughed and joked while they worked through the day. With the air raids at night, nobody could say they got a good night's sleep, but they seemed to be able work without showing any ill effects.

We were soon to load our cargo, our destination was home and that couldn't have been better for our crew. As soon as Frank had his papers from the ship he was away to the customs for clearance. We in the meantime had been getting the barge ready for sea and as soon as Frank got his foot over the rail it was, 'Let go, lads!' and then we were off down the docks to be ready for the early morning lockout.

That unfortunately was not to be. The dock head had been so badly damaged that we had to take our place in the queue to get out via the Albert Dock basin. The basin was full with river craft, and the lighters were completely jamming the area up. It took us nearly the whole day to get from the Albert Bridge to the lock head, and it had just gone dark in the evening when we at last cleared the pier heads and Frank took us across the river. He soon had us alongside the lighter roads, and we at least had a comfortable night's sleep.

In the morning, as always, it was time for the old kettle to go on. After a couple of mugs of tea and a few slices of bread and marmalade we were ready to slip away. The *Jean* had a so-called engine and Frank was usually able to get the thing going without too much trouble. That morning it decided to play up, and gave him a small fire to contend with. He soon had this under control but we were very late getting away from the roads. This engine had to have a lot of attention; it was petrol started, then changed over to run on paraffin. Once it was going it certainly pushed us along and with the ebb away we were able to have a very nice fast run down river.

Damage to the King George V bridge by the lock gates caused by the V.2. rocket on February 10th 1945.

The lofty spars of two barges tower defiantly over the Luftwaffe's bomb damage in the Surrey Docks.

I was able to get on with my chores like scrubbing around, and the old girl had soon lost all trace of the dock spoils. Frank had said that we would be going down to the Yantlet, if we were lucky enough to carry our daylight. We did manage to, and the *Lady Jean* was brought up in one of Frank's favourite anchorages to enjoy another peaceful night.

A few planes passed over us, no doubt on their way to the city, but none decided to stay in our area. Our start next morning, like most, was before dawn and cold with it. However, heaving short the anchor soon put some life into us. We used to put our backs into this chore to get it out of the way, and that day it meant we would soon be sailing homewards again. Frank was delighted with the way we lads had supported him in getting the barge on the move. Although the weather forecast the night before wasn't too good, he had said that he wanted to be going through the boom gate with the daylight. If we could do that we had a fair chance of getting through the Harwich boom before the evening's darkness.

As it happened we were able to do it quite easily. We had about a force six from the south-south-east, which couldn't have been better for us, for that's just how the old girl liked the weather. That wind was to stay with us for the next couple of days. At the end of the day's run we brought up just off Pin Mill. The Skipper was able to go home for the night as that was where he lived at the time.

Frank was back aboard the next morning at muster time. The engine started well for him and we began to get the anchor. He was pushing us ahead with the engine so we were able to whip the chain in fairly fast. We were soon at the 'short' stage when Frank broke the anchor out with the engine. As soon as that was done we had to nip it up as fast as we could. Frank motored us along up the river and, as he had already worked out, we went straight through the lock and up the dock into our berth.

We kept plying cargoes about, but I realised that one day I would lose my berth. It was for that reason that whilst I was mate of the *Lady Jean*, I was very attentive to what Frank did. If I didn't understand it at the time he was doing it, I would at the first chance ask him to explain the manoeuvre. He would gladly tell me and then I would pop down below and enter it into my notebook. I had been taught that to remember anything it was best to write it down and then read things up at night 'last thing'.

Our unloading went without a hitch and the third hand and I were soon busy filling up the water tanks and doing the usual jobs, such as sweeping out the hold. As soon as we were discharged, we turned to scrubbing round, and if it wasn't satisfactory Frank would soon be shouting.

After we had lain empty for a couple of days we heard the magic word 'orders', but Frank was fuming for we were to load the next cargo from Ipswich and take it up above bridges to Battersea. It seemed that no one ever wanted to do those trips, although the lad and I didn't really mind. Once we were loaded, it was then store up, and the usual clean up ready for away. We left Ipswich and ran down the Orwell to Shotley Stoneheaps, a well known anchorage for barges. We had the fishing gear out once we got to anchor and caught just enough to give us a feed. A very peaceful night was had by all until Frank gave us our early morning call. We jumped out of our canvas cots and soon had the paraffin primus stove going to boil the kettle for that first cup of tea.

We hove short and got the sail on her. We had a breeze from the nor'-nor'-west and Frank wanted to make full use of it. Soon we were slipping along out of the harbour, sent on our way by a cheery wave from the boom defence vessel.

We were drawing away from the land helped by a nice freshening wind as we got off shore, the breeze being fair for a smooth passage with a helpful tide. The day went very well and it was one of those when anyone would have liked our work. We tucked up nicely inside the West Shoebury buoy by evening, and after our stow up it was out with the fishing lines again. The fish were very kind to us and we soon had enough to hang in the rigging to give us food for a couple of days. Our fishing was usually very good as there was little commercial fishing going on anywhere. The fishermen were away on more important tasks, so nowhere was over-fished. After our evening meal, it was time for the Skipper's natter and then we were away to the old cot again.

The next day we knew was going to be a very busy one so we guessed that Frank would have us out very early. Sure enough, at about four-thirty we got the call to put the kettle on, and whilst that was on the go the anchor was hove up. We were underway by the time we were on our first cup of tea. It was one of Frank's bad moves to ask us to get the anchor up whilst the kettle was boiling! I don't think anyone can be expected to be at their best with an early start and no tea. Still, it was good to be underway again. With the engine going well and a full set of canvas we were making very good progress. The tide was to our advantage and Frank was sure that we would be in the Lower Pool at the end of the day.

Old Father Thames was really a fantastic river in those days and to be able to work on it was really great. All the craft working the Thames were going hell for leather to get in or out of the place. Most going out would return, but many others would be lost at sea and many good men with them. Mines were planted everywhere around our coasts. If the ships on the longer ocean runs managed to get clear of them, they then had to run the gauntlet of the German E-boats, and then further out the U-boats would be lying in wait. They had to have a great deal of luck to survive a round trip. All these thoughts were passing through my mind as we went up the river. I was glad that we were only classed as for the 'short sea trade' so hadn't quite so much to worry about.

Tugs, lighters and the big deep-sea craft were all working up on the tide and as we got further up the river it seemed to become very much busier. There was all the hooting going on as the ships and tugs gave the other craft warning of their intentions. Four blasts meaning to turn, followed by one meaning to starboard, two meaning to port; three told you that their engines were going astern. Another signal was the letter R - short long short hoots, meaning you could pass. You replied with one long and then one short if you intended to pass to starboard, or one long and two short if you were going to port. There were no VHFs in those days, and far fewer collisions. I learned all of that by just looking and listening as we worked the river. Frank told me there would be much more to learn if I was to achieve my ambition to become a barge master one day.

You could ill afford to look idly around if you had charge of the barge, the river was so busy you dare not relax. Frank kept pointing out anything that he thought would be useful to me. Included were the tide sets, the names of the various reaches and also the different dock entrances. I kept wondering to myself if I would ever be able to remember them all. Frank said that it could take a lifetime and I had by then begun to believe him.

Finally, after much grunting and groaning, the old engine got us up into the Lower Pool, and Frank swung the old girl head to tide. We then got a turn on the buoy just below Tower Bridge, and finally moored to it. The buoy was put there by the P.L.A.[1] for craft which had business up through the bridges. There was always a tug kept on station there, so no craft could really hit the bridge. If it looked likely, the tug was swiftly brought into action to provide assistance.

We had been very busy as we came up the river. The stay fall[2] had to be pulled up from the fo'c'sle, laid out along the deck and then passed around the barrel of the windlass three times ready for lowering all the barge's gear down to deck level to give us clearance through the bridges.

After the stay fall was made ready, the topmast was to be lowered. First we would heave the topmast heel rope tight using the mastcase winch. I would then nip aloft and remove the fid, a large iron pin going right through the heel of the topmast, allowing the topmast to be lowered. The crosstrees were also topped up out of the way, and we were then nearly ready to lower the main gear down. Finally we had to make sure the mast prop, which was simply a piece of six by three timber scooped out at one end to take the shape of the mast, was properly in place. It was stood on the after deck, near the main horse, ready to receive the mast.

Frank was soon surging the stay fall away round the windlass and the mast was on its way down. The sprit was soon to land on the saddle chock, the mainsail headrope then became slack as the gear was further lowered, and then the mast came down far enough for me to put the prop in and land the mast. We would then all jump about sharply to get some very good tackles and lashings around the mast. With all the traffic going past it would have been very easy for it to roll off the prop.

After that was all done, we were ready for the next day's flood tide to go on our way to Battersea. Again overnight the Jerries were very busy, but luckily

[1] The Port of London Authority. [2] The long wire rove through the stem blocks used to raise and lower down a barge's gear.

for us not too close to our buoy allowing the third hand and myself to get some sleep in preparation for what we expected to be another very busy day.

In the morning Frank asked if we had heard anything in the night, for it appeared that we had slept through some very heavy bombing. Still, after the wonders of a good breakfast, we were soon washed up and ready for action. Frank had good luck with the engine that time and we had soon slipped the buoy. We went out into the main stream of the tide and swung up so that soon we were flying along through Tower Bridge and London Bridge and then, in no time, we were off our berth. We swung round head into the tide and slipped alongside ready to unload.

Discharging at Battersea was no long drawn-out affair. As soon as we got ourselves alongside we had to heave the gear up out of the way so the dockers could commence unloading. We were all pleased with the rush as none of us wanted to hang about in the London area at that time.

The next day we had everything ready so that as soon as we floated we lowered the gear and cast off. As we had left the berth on the flood we had to push quite a bit of tide but Frank knew where to get into the slack. He had decided that we would go down to the Woolwich buoys, as we hadn't yet got any loading orders. This was just fine for the third hand and myself as we were sure to find a few of our mates down there who would help with the rerigging. Shortly after we had cleared the bridges the ebb tide came away so it wasn't long before it was time to round up at Woolwich, where we found ourselves alongside the *Jock*. Soon there was a willing crowd of helpers aboard so the third hand was sent below to make the tea.

The long haul to get the gear up was started, as we had got most things ready whilst coming down the river. With all the help the heaving was not stopped until we had lifted the gear back up into position. By that time the kettle was boiled and all hands could sit down for a well-earned cup of tea. With tea break over it was time for the topmast to go up. That was easy with all the help that we had. When it was nearly to its height, I had to nip aloft ready to pass the fid back through as the fid hole rose above the mast band. 'Stop!' I shouted to those on deck, and the topmast was lowered back down a little to rest on the iron cap.

All that remained was to clear up the ropes and bits and pieces. The willing hands stayed even after this was done, and some even stayed on to help with the scrubbing up. Frank passed comment that he had never seen the old girl recover from a trip up through the bridges so quickly. There was plenty of water being pulled up and sloshed about and the brooms and deck scrubbers were being wielded briskly. Nobody seemed to mind. All of these lads were just good mates prepared to help each other.

At such times as those when we had to wait for orders, Frank always used to help me to make use of the evenings. He would ask me to come aft after tea which usually meant that he was going to give me a lesson in chart work or something similar. I think it was also meant as a lesson for me to stay on board instead of going shore side to chase the girls and spend my money. Frank was a great believer in saving, and usually he would only allow us a very small advance on our wages. This meant that we always had some money to draw when we got back home, and very pleased we were too.

As day three came around so did our orders, and it was Ipswich empty for us and the *Jock*. As Frank boarded he ordered us to single up our lines, and put a couple of extra ropes on the *Jock* as we would be keeping him alongside down the river. Frank had brought some extra bread when he returned from the telephone, so we had no need to go ashore for stores. He then went below to start the engine. By the time our singling up was done he was ready for the off. We slipped from the other craft and were soon on our way. We even managed a bit of sail for the wind had been blowing hard from the south for quite a few days and we had all been saying it was a fair wind running to waste.

Once we were in the clear and going away down river, I went back aft to the wheelhouse. Frank told me that he was going down to the Yantlet for the night and hoped for an early start next day. *Jock* and ourselves would each be on our own anchor as it was blowing stronger. Frank and 'Spero' had decided that each barge would lie more quietly on its own.

'Spero' cast his eye at the old Ship and Lobster as we went past Denton, and I'm sure that would have done him if he had been on his own.

The Yantlet is a very well-known anchorage to the masters of any small craft wishing to shelter from winds from the east-south-east round to about the west-south-west. When we at last got the anchor down it was blowing about force six from the south. Frank said to give her plenty of chain as we didn't want to drag. The old *'Jean'* had very high bows, and used to sheer about when she was empty, putting additional strain on the anchor. Frank told me that before the war you would always make sure of a good riding light, so that if you did drag, others would see you. Being wartime, we were not allowed to show any lights at all or to be underway in the dark. We were very anxious to ensure that we did not drag. As we settled down for our tea we could hear the old girl roaring about over her anchor and she was really snatching and pulling everything tight, and there was quite a lot of groaning coming from the windlass.

After tea and our evening yarn, Frank told me to keep an ear open for any different noises, and he went aft for an early night. As the night wore on I wished that Frank hadn't said anything to me about the noises. I found great difficulty in sleeping, finding that I could really only catnap. I think I was looking forward to the daylight so we could get up and go. It had already been decided between the two Skippers that a daylight start would be about right, to allow the Thames boom defence vessel to have the boom gate open. With the very strong wind which we had, we would have to judge the gate right first time. We couldn't afford to be too early.

Nature decided to intervene. I had lain nearly all night waiting for something to happen, and it had to happen just as I was ready to settle down to that early morning sleep which wants to overtake you within a couple of hours of the time to get up. After just a few seconds I realised that all the noises had stopped except the roaring of the wind. I shouted to the third hand to get aft and put Frank in the picture. As soon as I got on deck I knew that we had a serious problem. The anchor chain was hanging limply down from the windlass against the stem so I knew the chain or something had parted. I rushed aft to make sure the Skipper was about and then got the kicking strap off the rudder so at least we would be able to steer when we had some sort of power.

Frank told me to organise a few cloths set in the mainsail and to set the foresail, and whilst the third hand was doing most of this I had lowered the leeboard. Frank got the engine going and we then had some sort of order. It was only then that the anchor chain was hove in and Frank told us to get the second anchor ready.

It began to seem as if it was going to be a long time before we were to get our brew-up. Our work went very well, and soon I was able to walk aft and tell Frank that all was okay forward, our spare anchor was shackled to the chain, and that the lad had gone below to get the tea going. 'Well done to the pair of you,' he said, adding that he would be more than glad to see the brew come along. He didn't have long to wait before the steaming mugs arrived.

Standing in the wheelhouse, Frank told me to catch hold of her, as he wanted to go forward and check things out. It was then that I looked at the compass and realised that we were holding the ship's head up river. I spoke to Frank about it and he told me he was gilling about until daylight. Until then I hadn't really noticed how dark it was. He told me that we would set the topsail sheet out, hook the mainsheet block to the traveller and set about half the mainsail. All that was done as Frank held us into the wind. He then took us right round to put us on a heading of east-north-east. The old 'Jean' seemed to know she had a fair wind and was heading home for she took off like a bat out of hell.

At last I was able to look astern to see if the *Jock* was about. Frank reckoned that as it was blowing like hell, 'Spero' would lie the day at the Yantlet. Before long we were passing through the boom gateway which rapidly disappeared astern with the wind increasing as the daylight came in. We talked about the life the lads on the boom gate vessel lived. What with the Jerry planes having a go and the weather they had to put up with, it was a tough job to do.

As we passed down towards the Blacktail Spit the third hand had decided that he would feed the contents of his guts to the fish. Frank told me to make him fast to the bow as he could see him going over the side with his vomit. I went along and very soon had him well secured!

Frank reckoned that as we would soon be getting some lee off the Barrow Sands that would be an ideal time for us to get some breakfast. So away to the

Lady Jean laden in the London River.

fo'c'sle I went and very soon had the tea made and took my nice mug-full aft to relieve Frank at the wheel.

He went below to cook himself a meal. The Skipper was, of course, always the first to eat. I would normally have to wait about an hour, and that day was no exception. By the time it was my turn to eat I was starved. Still, my bacon and eggs was well worth the wait. Obviously the very early start that day had something to do with my ravenous appetite.

Very soon I had devoured my eats and quickly did the washing up and got myself back on deck so as to get as much time as possible up there. I had never been at sea in that sort of weather before and being down below didn't do much for my own stomach.

When I got back on deck Frank told me that we were in for a full-blown gale, and before long it turned out that he was right. Frank himself didn't seem to be too concerned about this, for the old 'Jean' was a very well-found craft, and I had every faith in the ship and her Skipper. He was saying that if the breeze kept up we should be going round the Naze about slack water and that would do us very well. We were having a fast run even if it was very rough. Apart from that, the visibility was very good and things were going well. The wind seemed to have backed more to the south-east and we certainly had our full gale.

I had kept my eye on the third hand, as once we rounded the Naze, I had been able to speak to him. He told me to tell Frank that he would be leaving when we got in and that he wasn't going to sea any more. He did leave us and I recall that he went 'cross channel' and later on, deep-sea.

I think the third hand was all wrong when he complained about the 'Jean's' rolling, for she rolled no more than a lot, and much less than others. The old saying about timber built vessels, 'All fast ships leak' we certainly proved to be true that day.

After we had rounded the Naze and run down to the north-east as far as Frank wanted, we then had to gybe over. This meant quite some work for us. First I had to let go the lee rolling vang, then we hove in the sprit until it was more or less centred. The mainsheet was hove in tight as well and a turn taken around the main horse toe, after which Frank was able to gybe the Lady Jean with the minimum of fuss in the strong wind.

As soon as we were round on the new course and squared away for the harbour, Frank gave me the wheel. Whilst we were running towards the boom he went below to start the engine ready for the river. As we ran in through the boom gateway Frank appeared back on deck, and exchanged the usual cheery waves with those on the boom vessel.

The Skipper decided to keep the sail on her until we reached Collimer Point, and then stow up. Once we got up to Pin Mill, Frank eased us into a good spot and the anchor plunged down into the water. We then went aft and lowered the barge boat into the river.

Frank was soon ready to leave and, as he lived just ashore at Pin Mill, he was home soon after we landed him on the causeway. He told us at what time to pick him up the next morning and we made our way back to the barge to get a peaceful night's sleep.

Next day we had a good run up river under power. Frank had already got our orders before coming afloat, and we were going to load malting barley again. There must have been a lot of good whisky drinkers somewhere to need the amount of barley that was going up to London. We suspected that the military had quite a lot of it sent to them, and no doubt the nobs had some way of getting hold of their share.

I knew that my days aboard the *Lady Jean* were numbered, as Frank had told me the prospect of the barge running down to King's Lynn. I wouldn't be allowed to go as mate at my age as the insurance wouldn't cover the barge. We knew the shipping manager was looking for someone in the proper age bracket, for the old '*Jean*' really needed someone with more power to his elbow. I suppose I put more strain on to an ageing Master, although he was as strong as a horse. However, he really had the right to someone more experienced and physically stronger than me.

When the '*Jean*' went back to proper coasting Frank would also need a mate who was a qualified watch keeper. It really came as no surprise when one day a few trips later Frank came aboard and said that they had got this chap who was twice my age, and very much more experienced than me, who they were going to ship as mate. Frank and I were able to part on very amicable terms. He had given me my introduction to proper chart work, and kept me interested when we had to lie about. I do think that with the effort Frank put into it, he really got a kick out of teaching me. Frank had told me that most of the lads didn't want to learn anything more than the everyday run-of-the-mill work, and that it made a change to find someone who wanted to learn.

I had given much thought to the sailing barge at this time and even then could see that their numbers were dwindling and the crews becoming a dying breed. I was fortunate to learn all I had from Frank, as I had now acquired my basic navigation and a good introduction to seamanship at its best. And so it was that I had to take my departure from the *Lady Jean* with the good wishes and blessing of the Master.

A typical dockland scene in the early 1940s. Francis & Gilders' *George Smeed* loads South African maize, and one of The London & Rochester Trading Company barges lies beyond. The merchant ship's after gun sits menacingly overseeing the loading of the dumb lighters and sailing barges.

Chapter VI
CAN YOU SPLICE, SON?

The shipping manager had said there would probably be a berth in a week or two's time in another one of Paul's craft. At that time I declined his offer as I had heard of another berth that I was interested in. I had decided that the barge by the share had better see me again, for I realised that the locals, mainly Pauls and Cranfields, nearly always went to the same places. The share barges were the coasters that had to go where they were sent. I hadn't very far to roam, for one such craft lay at Pin Mill, and there I found the old *George Smeed*.

The old *'Smeed'*, for old she was, had had a nasty crunch into the concrete north pier at Yarmouth harbour. They had to get the cargo out in a terrific hurry as the starboard bow had sort of caved in and she was taking on water. Flour was very short at that time, as we were still at war with Germany, so the cargo could not be allowed to spoil

The entrance at Yarmouth was known to be very difficult for sailing craft to enter on their own, so nine times out of ten the Master would take the tug. To go in under sail alone, the weather had to be perfect or so bad that the tug wouldn't come out for you.

It appears that the harbour tug had picked the barge up all right on that occasion. As they got into the eddy tide at the entrance the tug was going hell for leather in the correct line for the centre of the harbour. It was at that time that the *'Smeed'* took a run for the north pier. The Skipper, Jerry Mann, said that there was a fair swell running and one just picked the *'Smeed'* up and threw her at the pier. The tug should and would have pulled her clear, but with a resounding crack the towrope parted. Fortunately they were far enough inside the harbour to allow them another chance. As Jerry and his mate fought to get the broken towrope back on board, the tug Skipper slid his craft back alongside. The crew of the tug were able to help get another rope secured and hauled the *'Smeed'* to the ABC[1] wharf. The crane went straight into the forward hold to whip out the cargo. With the holds clear, Jerry was able to see that the old girl was not leaking whilst empty.

The owners had decided that the best yard around for the sort of repair the barge needed was Webb's at Pin Mill. They put Jerry and his mate on yard pay so they hadn't to worry about pushing the old girl too hard to get there.

Within a couple of days the weather was good enough for Jerry to order the tug and get a pull out. He enjoyed a good pull clear out into a fresh northeast wind, so the tug was dropped and the barge squared away for a pleasant run to Harwich and on up the Orwell to Webb's yard at Pin Mill.

[1] The Aerated Bread Company.

The Skipper, Jerry Mann, was swearing enough over the damage, as it was proving to be very costly to him. The money that he would collect whilst on the yard would be a pittance. Indirectly, all these events lined me up for the berth. Jerry told me that his mate George had decided to get himself married and go as Master himself. Jerry said that George was a very experienced man, and that nobody could afford to be married on a mate's wage.

Transport for me when I was ashore in those days was the good old bicycle, so I got mine out and made my way down to Pin Mill, first ringing Francis and Gilders at Colchester. The gent in the office there had told me all about the berth. He seemed to think that I could be lacking in experience but said that the Master should decide.

As to first impressions, I don't think I did too well. As well as being a lad on the small side, I think Jerry was eyeing me up as likely to cause him a lot of extra hard work for himself. I'm sure lady luck must have been on my side in the form of Jerry's wife, Vi. After a nice cup of tea produced by her, and a lot of questioning by Jerry, Vi more or less told Jerry to give me a chance.

Being on the hard at Pin Mill was to turn out to be a major test for me. Jerry had said that if I could splice the towrope the job would be mine. That in itself was to present no problems as in my very early days as a Sea Scout I had learnt the art of rope splicing. This rope turned out to be a bit different, being of about a nine-inch girth, and a bass[1] rope at that. It also had to have a large thimble put into the splice. All this I did and at the finish it gave me great satisfaction. But the interesting bit was yet to come. Jerry's joke, as soon as I had finished and he had checked and said 'Well done,' was, 'now, what about the wire?'

I must admit that at the time I only had a very vague idea about the art of wire splicing. Jerry could only be described as an expert. I also found that he could get anything over to me, so that made him a good teacher in my book. He was also able to give me confidence in my work.

Our towing gear was very heavy owing to the nature of its use. Jerry said he would do the splice but with me assisting him so that I could learn how to do it myself. We had a heavy thimble to splice into the wire, which meant that we had to bowse the wire around the thimble. Under the guidance of Jerry we put the necessary whippings on the wire and also the strands as we peeled them back ready for the actual splice to start.

After Jerry had done the locking tuck we could hang the eye up and, by pulling the standing part taut using a tackle, we were able to do what we call 'run the wire', drawing the spike down through the wire, followed by the strand until it was finished. All the strands were dealt with in the same way and the final product was called a Liverpool splice. To get to that stage was really all down to Jerry, although he gave me some of the credit. I was very pleased with the end result and Jerry trusted me with the task of cutting the ends off and clouting the splice down.

[1] A coarse natural fibre, originally from lime trees.

Finally he asked if I knew the rhyme that went with this work and I replied 'Worm and parcel with the lay, turn and serve the other way.' I think he was suitably impressed!

Whilst all the splicing was going on, Jerry's wife kept the teapot going. She was also cleaning and preparing the cabin ready for a paint out, most of which she did herself.

The starboard bow had more or less to be rebuilt. I was fortunate to be on the yard whilst it was going on, for old Ted Webb and his gang of shipwrights, most of them relatives, were the best.

Ted took the first few days to decide on his working methods, and also to prepare a list of materials. Once that had been sorted out, Ted and his men got to work. One of the first things they did was to surround the starboard bow area with the staging they would need to work from. That task was quickly done and soon the sound of hammers and jemmy bars could be heard from early morning to late evening.

The old 'Smeed' had been rebuilt in her earlier years and had been 'doubled' with an additional skin. That was a common practice, but it made the repairs more complicated

We were aware during those first few busy days, that the end of the war with the Germans seemed to be getting closer. One day, after I had cycled to Pin Mill, Jerry told me it was all over and that I could have the day off. He had even subbed me my day's pay, which at that time was seven shillings and four pence and rounded it up to the sixpence ($37^1/_2$ p). That was the going rate for Mates in Francis and Gilders' barges in those days. I jumped on my bicycle and with a cheery wave was soon off whistling a merry tune. The town of Ipswich celebrations had already started by the time I dumped the bike at home and put the old glad rags on. Knowing where my chums were likely to be, I soon joined them, and for young and old the beer was flowing much too freely.

As the evening wore on, the mood of the crowd seemed to change, and the singing on the Corn Hill in the town centre turned to near riots, and the police were called out. Even with their loudspeakers going, the rowdy crowd took no notice, so the police came out swinging riot batons, and gave us in the crowd some good clouts to make us turn away. I had a very heavy bruise on my elbow with the imprint of my jersey in it, and it was with me for quite some time after the celebrations were over.

Although we had gone a bit wild, I don't think anyone was locked up, and I think a good time was had by all. I would assume that many millions of people who resumed work the following day were suffering from a thick head. I think that I had a good start over most of them in recovering. I had first to cycle a good seven miles to get to work and then when I arrived the air was fairly fresh and very sobering down on the hard at Pin Mill.

When I arrived Jerry told me we were going to help with the barge repairs. I was very pleased to hear this as it gave me an opportunity to learn about the practical side. I hadn't realised, until we got involved, that as each old plank had been removed it was carefully taken up to the old lean-to at the top of the causeway above the tide line. There the lads took a template of each plank, marking up any irregularities on the template. Using this technique it followed that when the new boards were cut and shaped they were more or less a fit. Ted's lean-to was just a few scaffold poles lashed together and a few old tarpaulins tied around them. It was there all the timber was shaped up ready to go into the barge.

Our berth at Pin Mill was on Ted's blocks, where the barge sits on large timbers about three feet above the hard level. She would only float on top of the spring tides enabling the shipwrights to work away on the lower planks whilst the neap tides were about.

Ted gave me the job of digging out six holes in the hard. Each had to be about three foot deep and alongside the barge's starboard bow. As each hole was dug out I had to drop a post, about six inches round, into the hole and tie a line around the post at deck level. I then had to backfill the hole around the base of the post so the whole thing became solid. Ted then gave me some small block and tackles to be made fast to the top of the posts, led across over the fore hatch and made off on the port bow. Then it was the turn of Ted's men to follow on with the first of the new planks, and for me to gather firewood.

It had been explained to me that they would be putting this old large bath down alongside our bow, and that my job would be to keep the water in it on the boil. I had a regular job going up and down the hard, gathering up all the odd bits and pieces of wood the shipwrights had left in the lean-to, and carting them down to stoke the fire under the bath.

The bath, about half full of water, had been placed next to the bow of the barge. Although it took an age to get it to the boil, it was no trouble once it got there. Two planks had been brought down to the barge, one had been slipped into the boiling water in the bath, sacking was stuffed in over it and then it was left like this for about three hours before the real work started.

Bearing in mind that this plank was of sorted timber and already cut and shaped, the men had every confidence that it would fit. As it came out of the bath the steamed end was to go up against the stem. It was passed down inside the posts and the aft end was lined up. Ted gave the word and the spikes were driven home at the bow. The tackles were then hove in and wedges were driven between the posts and the new plank, and slowly the it was forced round into position.

It was hard to believe the curvature that it was possible to obtain, particularly as the shipwrights made light of that side of their work. The second plank went in just as well and with great confidence shown by all. Ted had told Jerry that two planks a day would be our lot, the way the tides were.

So the work slowly progressed, and with the ring of the adze and the hammers going all day, the first skin was finally hammered home. Next came the tar and horsehair which were put on over the first skin. With the outer skin, the edges of the planks were treated with the tar and horsehair mixture. The work went on with some days being long and others very short, each being dictated by Ted and the state of the tides.

That it would be a long job was known when the old '*Smeed*' first went on the yard. Jerry and Vi, who had finished painting the cabin out, had gone away for a holiday. I had been home each night.

Eventually the day came around when we realised the finish was in sight. Jerry ordered up stores for us from our Colchester yard. These included paints, paraffin and the like, and a few new ropes. Then the day arrived when Ted said, 'That's it Jerry, you can go.' Jerry walked ashore to see if we had any orders - we could only hope that there was something about. There was a reasonable chance of getting something as, with Francis & Gilders, when a 'share barge' came off the yard it had a top priority to load. Jerry came back aboard with a spring in his step and told me, 'We've got a doddle of a job for your first trip, mate.' We had to go to Felixstowe dock and load flour from there and deliver part of the cargo to Southend and part to Grays.

We had to wait another couple of days for enough tide to get off the blocks, but as soon as we had water Jerry was off. I was then to learn about 'Jerry the mad one', as some called him. We only had a short run to Felixstowe and we were even able to sail into the piers, and nearly to our berth. But we had to let go the anchor to stop her and, as she swung to it, I had a line away to the mill side. We were then able to heave the anchor home and the barge alongside. As we moored up, the mill foreman said to Jerry that they were going to start us straight away to get us finished on the next day's tide. The mill's own craft, *The Miller*, was due there on the following tide.

The motor barge *The Miller* belonged to the Felixstowe Mill owners.

We started loading aft first, which was the usual way, and that allowed us to try the pumps aft, and it also saved having to walk forward if you had to pump out during the night. We got a very good start to our loading, checking on the pumping as we loaded. While we were loading aft we had no problems, but when we started the forward hold the next morning, it was certainly a different tale.

We had got about half the forward hold down when Jerry realised that we were making water fast. He started dropping all the ash and dust from our fire that he could find over the bow. The idea was that as the ash sank it would be drawn into the stem area by the leak and so helped to seal the bow up. It was not a completely watertight job, but it was good enough to allow us to keep ahead of the water level with the pump.

Jerry said that the planking would tighten up once it was immersed. We had got a long way to go and that meant we had a lot of pumping to do. We started battening down and finished as soon as the last bag of flour went into the forehold. Jerry went ashore and signed for the cargo, and then it was let go and away.

We had a fair breeze from the north and Jerry was determined to make the best use of it. After about a couple of hours' sailing it became clear that we were making water fairly fast and Jerry's wife and I were kept very busy on the pumps. We had an uninterrupted sail to Southend. Although we didn't make it to our berth, when we got there Jerry put us ashore on the sand and we were able to leave the pumps alone for a few hours as the tide left her. After we floated it was just a matter of a couple of hours pumping before we got into our berth. Once again we took the ground. As the tide ebbed it wasn't long before we were again able to forget about the pumps for a few more hours and get some sleep.

Next morning there was shouting for us to get uncovered as we had overslept. It didn't take us long to get the forehold uncovered. A couple of hours later and we were down among wet flour, which Jerry had already told me we would have to take back to Felixstowe at no cost to anyone. We were not going to get very rich out of that cargo. We got rid of our one hundred tons of cargo to Southend. We then had to sail to Grays. As the leak was then above the water, our trip up the river to Grays went much better. The only sad thing was that Vi was going home for a time, and we would certainly miss her.

After the flour had been discharged at Grays it was a very sad sight in the hold. There were about two tiers of bags of wet flour all over the ceiling[1] and I came to realise just how much water had been sloshing about. We would have been in a bad way if we had experienced a rough trip. Jerry organised some of the Grays' lads to get most of the wet bags into the middle of the hold, which would make it easier for us when we got back to Felixstowe. It was a good job it was all casual labour, as the London Dockers wouldn't have touched it at all.

The run back down to Felixstowe caused us no problems, except the misery of knowing that we were doing it for nothing. The trip was good and the discharge of the wet flour very quick, so maybe our luck was beginning to change.

[1] The 'ceiling', possibly derived from 'sealing', or so called because it is above the 'floor' timbers, is the floor of the hold. With loose cargoes such as grain it was vital that this floor was 'sealed' to prevent the cargo getting into the bilge and blocking the pumps.

The *'Smeed'* under topsail, foresail and full main, and without her bowsprit shipped.

I had begun to realise that the *George Smeed* was a much easier barge to work than the *Lady Jean*, particularly as the gear was so much smaller and lighter. Jerry was a very wiry man and also a great deal younger than Frank, so in the general running about getting the craft underway Jerry was a great help to me.

Getting out of Felixstowe dock on that occasion, however, gave us a few problems. The wind was blowing right in when we were ready to leave. The motor boat that was usually about, and would have hauled us off, was away having a new engine fitted. That meant that we had a very long heave with the dolly wire from our berth, right out to the pier end, before we were able to spring away. Once beyond the jetty end we were in the grip of the ebb tide which set us down clear. As we set off on the port tack the old '*Smeed*' lay to the good fresh breeze. She was soon showing Felixstowe a clean pair of heels as we made our way up river to go back on the yard at Pin Mill for Ted to take another look at our leak.

After Ted had taken the stem scarphing piece off it revealed where the trouble was, as water had got down behind it. Ted and his shipwrights soon had this caulked up and the stem scarphing piece restored. Ted again declared us fit to go and pressed a fiver each to Jerry and me and told us to have a drink on him, so we didn't really lose out too much on the trip after all.

Fingringhoe Mill at the top of the Roman River; the *George Smeed* deep laden under the elevator.

Coming off the yard put us next in turn for orders again. We had to get ourselves up to Colchester Hythe to load a cargo of grit for Bow Creek. Jerry laughed and said that it was a cargo which would test the repair.

Jerry and I were pleased that we hadn't to do any pumping as we got the cargo aboard. Then Jerry explained that the '*Smeed*' was known as a hog-backed vessel when loaded with a dead-weight cargo such as this. This really meant that the barge sort of dropped in the middle with the cargo in, and when empty dropped at the ends. She would be tight when loaded and likely to leak on a hard passage when empty.

Our trip up was a very easy one and as soon as we had got into Bow Creek and berthed, the grab was brought into action, whipping the cargo out. Jerry was able to nip off home for a few hours and also have time to pop into the London office to collect a nice fat sub which gave me the chance to have a few quiet beers in celebration.

After I had made several trips with Jerry he decided that we could afford to employ a third hand who would be paid out of our share of the freight money. Jerry was thinking of the tax that we would save, and so thought that we could give a lad a start. When next we were in Felixstowe Dock and I went home for the night, I was told to sort a third hand out, if any were about. Crews of any rank were no problem in Ipswich and I was able to go into the Sailor's Rest and get hold of a third hand based on 'gut feeling'. I told him to report aboard the next day when Jerry would hire or not. I say with 'gut feeling' for that was the first person that I was to give a job to.

The first trip with the third hand was to prove a disaster for Jerry, who had decided to start the lad. His first trip was to be empty from Felixstowe to London after we had finished unloading our grain into the mill. Soon the last wedge was driven in the hatch coaming and the lashings were all secured.

Mitch, in his little motor boat, was telling Jerry that there was a lot of swell outside, but Jerry was not too bothered about it. He had already told me that we would get away as soon as possible to get up swin as far as we could before the next ebb came away. We had a very strong wind from the south and the Skipper's intention was to push us to the limit. Whilst we had the flood tide we made fair progress. Jerry said that, with luck, once the tide came away it would set off the sands and provided the wind stayed from the south we should be able to make something of it. Jerry's idea was right, but the wind was really blowing and the *'Smeed'* was getting a hammering. When we got just above the South Whitaker buoy we were down to topsail sheet and about half mainsail and going to leeward like a crab. Then Jerry said, 'No good, mate, we'll have to bear away and go up Whitaker.' Once we arrived up at Shore Ends, the anchor was buried in the seabed and we were all stowed up, and it was only then that my thoughts turned to the third hand. I went below to light the riding light and was met by a terrible smell which was, of course, our seasick shipmate who we hadn't seen since leaving Felixstowe!

After a day and a half had passed, though I'm sure there was no abatement in the weather, Jerry was stomping about and saying he thought that we ought to be getting underway. I realised that Jerry wasn't smoking, as he had run out of baccy. My few fags had long gone and so I went along for'ard, for I knew our third hand had bought hundreds of cigarettes with him, and he would not be needing any for a while. The smell was really unbearable but I didn't intend to stay down there long. It took but a few moments before I found the two hundred packs of Craven 'A' cigarettes. I went aft and realised that Jerry had gone to the cabin. I lit the first fag, lay near the hatch and blew the smoke down below. It was but just a few moments before Jerry got a whiff of the smoke and took a flying leap across the cabin on to the ladder. I had tried to get out of sight, but after he poked his head outside the hatchway he soon spotted me and the air went blue. Jerry thought that I had been holding out on him. I slung him a couple of packets, and explained where they had come from. He was soon a happy man again after he had puffed a couple away, and decided he was content to lie up the rest of the day there.

On our third day there Jerry was ready to do battle with the elements again. We were able to get as far as the South Shoebury Buoy after one hell of a trip. There, we had to bring up ready until the low water and then try and make more of our passage. But alas, the *'Smeed'* was not having any of it and although we had started to heave in the anchor before low water it was nearly three hours into the flood by the time we got it on the bow. After a couple of boards under way, Jerry said, 'We're not doing anything at all, mate, we'll have to go to anchor again.'

What he didn't say until we had turned and started to run away from the weather was that we would have to run back over the top of the sands to Shore Ends again to get some sort of lee. The sea was very short and furious so I imagined we would both be very pleased to see the West Buxey Buoy. In that weather, with as much wind as we had, we were not very long in getting there. As we went just to the west of it, I'm sure the *'Smeed'* seemed to say, 'There, I told you so.'

We had started a run[1] in the topsail and Jerry thought that then was the time to do the repair. The old girl came and lay head to wind and there was I sitting up astride the mainsail head rope near the peak of the sprit, with Jerry tending the topsail sheet whilst I did the stitching. After an hour or so up there I was certainly pleased to regain the deck.

[1] Run - a tear or split, sometimes in the sail cloth, sometimes a failed seam between the strips of cloth which make up the sails.

The *George Smeed* with a 'stack' of timber, her mainsail brailed to the sprit and bowsprit steeved up.

About half an hour later, after we had consumed a couple of mugs of tea each, and I'd recovered from my hair-raising experience aloft, Jerry calmly said, 'Right, mate, let's get at it.' I'm sure the fags and the repairs had given his batteries a recharge.

Whilst we had been doing the sail repair, a rather nasty squall had hit us. The wind had shot round from the north-west, and that meant off the land. The swell would soon go down and that's why Jerry was so keen to get at it. The rest of our trip could be described as bearable. Jerry was like a bear with a sore head because of the time that we had taken so far. There was no money for it and the saga of the third hand, who didn't surface until we got into Gravesend Reach, added to the misery. As soon as Jerry saw him he was told to get his bags packed and not to do any work as he didn't intend to pay him any wages. After we had arrived at Erith, the lad was paid off with just the price of the cigarettes I had nicked and a few bob for his bus fare home.

Alan, our new third hand, was to turn out to be a very good find. He and I got on very well and I think that between us we gave Jerry the crew that he required.

Before long we had done quite a few trips together, and we were lying at Erith once again waiting for orders. Jerry came and gave his usual call for us to go and pick him up off the quay and said that we had got orders to go to the Surrey Docks to load tree trunks for Maldon. Jerry also said that he hadn't been well for a couple of days but thought he was over the worst, probably the flu. At any rate, we had a fair run up the river and after he had got us to the pier head he was able to go home. Alan and I were able to do the rest; get us into the dock and book on to the ship. Loading took place a couple of days later.

I had rung Jerry, but got Vi, the first night that we started to load. She told me that he was a lot worse. On the second evening, when I rang to say that we had loaded, I was again speaking to Vi. She told me Jerry had said to try and get her down to Erith. We would incur extra dock dues if we lay where we were for more than three tides. After I told the third hand what we were about he said, 'Well at least he trusts us!'

When I had sorted the paperwork out and got back on board, Alan had entered into the spirit of things and had got the barge squared up. We just had to let go from the ship's side and, the way the wind was, where we had to push in front of the lighters that were bound outward. Half the lightermen were not even with their craft, so we never had any bother from them. We were able to get out with the next locking, so didn't waste any time. When we got to the outer pier head one of the local toshers came for a couple of the lighters, and we bartered a carrier bag of sugar for a tow down as far as Blackwall Point.

The wind was fair and giving us a very good start, and by the time it came for us to let go, all our sails were set and filling well. The old Tosher cast us off as he bore away for Bow Creek. Getting down to Erith was no problem and as we approached the ballast wharf buoy one of the friendly police boats gave us a push, which helped us to moor up easily. It appeared they had run out of tea, so with some of our tea chest sweepings we were able to thank them.

We went ashore to see Jerry, but he was too ill to see us. Vi made us very welcome and insisted that we had lunch there. In all honesty that's why we had made our visit about that time. As far as Jerry was concerned, it didn't look very good for a few days yet and Alan and I were a bit down as we strolled back on board. After lying there a couple more days the wind had gone steadily round to the south-south-east and was about force four. I went round to Jerry's to give him my daily report and told him of the weather. I don't think he was delirious at the time but he said, 'Why don't you take her down?' He said it so calmly that I just said thank you, and got out of the house as fast as possible before he could change his mind.

As soon as I got back on board I said to Alan, 'We're off!'

I think for a few seconds he thought I had gone crazy, but after I had assured him about what Jerry had said, he just grinned and said, 'When do we start?' I said, 'Now.' The tide was only about an hour's ebb and we had the canvas billowing out and the old '*Smeed*' turning away down the river on passage seaward to Maldon.

Running down river was just great and I was tempted to keep going, but then I thought of it being dark around the Whitaker and the Spitway, and thought better of it. I said to Alan that we would be bringing up at the Yantlet for a few hours kip. We anchored and I left the deck, with a light southerly wind and a wonderfully clear sky, to turn in. I'm sure Jerry would have kept going and brought up where the barge decided to stop, should the wind have fallen fine. I lay down and wondered if I had done the right thing. Waking a couple of hours before the alarm was due to go off, I suppose I smoked a day's quota of cigarettes, probably due to apprehension of my new responsibilities and what the day might bring, I went up on deck and found a light breeze from the north-west. I felt somewhat disappointed, but we could have had it a lot worse.

I'm convinced to this day that we had the weather god with us, for the wind backed and came out of the south again, and so it held until we were up and over the Spitway and off Mersea Quarters. Then we had a spell becalmed before the wind made in from the south-east, which was about the best that we could have for Maldon. We ran right up to the promenade where we ran out of water and took the ground. As we stowed up, the little motor boat came down and stood by, so that as we floated he was able to pull us up to our berth ready for discharge. Alan and I had a good celebration ashore that evening. We also had nearly a week lying on the quay on demurrage[1] before it was our turn to start discharging, after which our Skipper, by then recovered, came back aboard.

Our next run was to be another empty hold, so no pay, back up to the ballast wharf buoy. It always seemed like home again as we put Jerry ashore for orders. After the third day Jerry came along with his usual shout and Alan went ashore to fetch him. He gave us the good news that we would be going up to the Victoria Docks to load a cargo of grain for Yarmouth. He went ashore overnight and returned at low water next day. I had already singled up ready to go, but we never had an air of wind. We lay there until at last one of the toshers came near us and Jerry was able to hail him and he rounded up.

The intentions of the tosher were very clear. They said they would give us a jerk until we got a breeze, and so the pound of tea sweepings was passed over. The tosher then went forward ready to sort us out. The toshers always passed their rope to the lighter or whatever they towed. I made the end of the rope fast to our bow cleat.

As I took the bight of the rope forward the tosher went full ahead, as he would with a lighter, but we had high rails and the rope had to lead from the forward snatch. I found myself with my leg trapped between the starboard rail and the towrope, being slowly but surely turned over the side as I screamed my head off.

Hearing my shouts, Jerry had started to run for'ard, but the mate of the tosher, also aware of my plight, had thrown his engine out of gear. The tow

---

[1] A compensation payment to the vessel when the consignee is not able to unload the cargo within an allotted time.

rope slacked up and I fell over the side on the point of passing out through the pain. In record time the crew of the tosher had me out of the river and passed me back on board the old 'Smeed'.

As soon as I was put back on board, and seen to be not too much the worse for wear, it was decided to carry on. The tosher pushed open the throttle and we soon made progress with the tide and the tow in our favour. As we were making our way up the river, so the pain in my leg was increasing, and the swelling.

Once the tosher had put us alongside the pier head at the Albert Dock entrance I was carted away in an ambulance to hospital. Jerry sent Alan with me and told him to stay with me, unless they decided to keep me in. After the tests at the hospital, the Doctors decided that I had nothing broken, but my thigh muscles had been pulled down towards the knee. They dressed the leg in a fancy sort of material and then told me that I would need to rest it for a few days. Alan got the hospital to arrange our transport to the Victoria Dock, but we had some trouble convincing the dock gate cop that we were genuine crew. He did finally let us through and so we were able to get to where Jerry had told us to wait for him and the barge. He hadn't arrived when we got there, but one of our firm's fleet was alongside so we were able to go aboard for a cup of tea and to await the arrival of the 'Smeed'.

Old Joe, the Skipper of the *Lady Helen*, was not just to give me that cup of tea. So that Jerry and the lad could have some time at home, during the week we lay alongside him waiting for cargo, he saw to all my needs.

Evenings were the worst times lying like that for, had I been fit and able, I would have been ashore with the lads. Canning Town was a very lively spot in those days, but some of old Joe's yarns were much better than the ones I would have heard ashore, and so the time passed.

I was able to hobble about a bit by the fifth day, but Jerry gave me a bit of verbal when he came by one day and told me that I must keep the leg rested. He also got Joe to sort me out and make sure that I did as he said.

At last it was our turn to load and that went without a hitch. Jerry and Alan were aboard again so I was the tea boy. It turned out that Jerry had done some thinking whilst at home and had decided that he would act as mate for the trip. This would allow me to sit on a box and do the shouting once we had left the dock. I knew that it wouldn't last for long, but it was a nice gesture.

We had an easy run down the river. The old 'Smeed' seemed to know we wanted a quiet trip and going seaward she behaved herself. That in itself should have told us that it couldn't last! We didn't stop at all until we got down to the West Mouse and the wind finally died away. As we were stemming the tide we came to a stop and so down went the anchor. There was no real stow up, we just dropped the foresail and put a few loose turns round it, the head of the topsail was lowered and pulled down snug on its gaskets, and once we had the main brails tight we were ready for a couple of hours

Francis & Gilders' *Lady Helen* seen leaving Colchester, behind the little motor boat.

down on the locker. Jerry noticed that the barometer was falling rapidly and muttered 'I don't like the look of that.'

About four hours after we had brought up would have been the ideal time for us to get underway, the time of high water. But the high water puff, as we used to say, came first. It was about an hour before the top of the tide, and we had been rolling about very badly. Jerry decided that we would get underway and make use of the weather. The wind had shot out to the south-east so we had a fair slant. As the sands to windward of us were then covered there was quite a lot of swell running. We had plenty of water coming aboard.

Jerry sent me below to make sure that I didn't get my dressings wet. Once again I had been reduced to the rank of tea boy. Running down toward the Spitway, Jerry had long since decided that we would keep outside the Gunfleet Sands as the wind was still coming at us from the south-east. It seemed no time at all before we had got down to the north-east Gunfleet buoy and so it became make your mind up time for Jerry. He could bear away and go for the safety of Harwich, or he could keep going. I knew Jerry was very concerned about the falling glass, but the urge to get there won and we carried on.

The *George Smeed* being flare sided, was at her worst when it came to running. The swells used to come aboard and the leeboards used to take a hammering when the slop got in behind them. Approaching Orford Ness, with the weather worsening and the seas building, Jerry had called me up on deck to assist him to steer. Alan was doing the sail adjustments to make the old girl as easy as possible. It was the middle of a very dark night and the sea was running with a bad streak in it. One sea bigger than the rest climbed inside the starboard leeboard and the toggle[1] parted, leaving the leeboard hanging on by the preventer and the pendant. Over and over again, the leeboard swung away from the barge and surged back alongside with a crash, whilst Jerry and Alan fought to control it After several unsuccessful attempts to bowse it alongside Jerry decided that we would let the preventer go and tow the leeboard astern of the barge. Although it made steering even more difficult, it enabled us to continue on our way.

We arrived off Yarmouth and hove to on the starboard tack, there to stow up and await the tug to come for us. The conditions were ideal for us to sail in, as it was high water slack, but without the leeboard we needed, Jerry wouldn't take the chance. The tug, the *George Jewson*, soon appeared out of the harbour and, taking our towrope, headed for the pier heads. Whilst under tow we were able to do a full harbour stow before reaching the ABC wharf, and prepare for discharge. Once alongside we retrieved and re-hung our starboard leeboard, so the old 'Smeed' would be ready for sea again.

I had the condition of my leg checked at Yarmouth Hospital. It appeared that the Connaught Hospital staff had done a really good job on it and the doctors passed me as fully fit again.

[1] Retaining pin at the head of the leeboard where it pivots.

Our next orders were for London empty to the Victoria Dock to load a cargo of grain for Ramsgate, a new destination for me. Our passage from Yarmouth to London was about the best trip that I can ever remember. The tug had towed us clear of the harbour and then pulled our head into the north-east, and held us there as we got the topsail and mainsail set. Then they pulled us before the wind, and we let go the towrope, set the foresail, and were away. Our big lightweight jib was set up to windward and we had a fast non-stop run from Yarmouth to the Albert Dock entrance. The only thing that marred the trip was that Alan gave his notice. Apparently he had been offered a mate's job, which he would have been a fool to turn down.

After we had lain a few days awaiting our cargo the ship worker told me they would be loading us early evening. This meant that they would be well paid for the work. We didn't mind the evening loading either, for there was extra money to be made. The only thing I had against it was that many of the dockers who should have been there were probably in the pub outside the dock, but nobody seemed to check up on them. With Jerry at home it meant that I had all the trimming to do myself. Still, the *George Smeed* was a good barge to load, normally taking about a couple of hours to fill, so I could cope.

Next morning Jerry and, to my surprise, Vi came on board fairly early, but without the intention of going out of the dock. The weather was no go, blowing a gale of wind and raining like hell, so all we did was to make ready for sea and get a few stores in. After a couple of games of cards, Jerry and Vi made the trip home to Erith again.

Later that afternoon Fred Smy in the motor barge *Atrato* offered to give me a tow down the docks and I jumped at it. He kept us alongside and we had a good clear trip even though it was damp, because all the lightermen and toshers had gone home to get out of the weather. That evening I was able to go ashore to get myself a nice pint and let Jerry know the good news. It meant that we didn't have to start till eleven o'clock the next morning. The day began a lot better weatherwise than the one before and again Vi was with Jerry when he got aboard. We were swinging on the outside pier heads when they arrived as I had taken the chance and went out with the *Atrato* as Fred had offered to pull us through the locks. As Jerry didn't show up before he was ready to go on down the river, we didn't get a longer free tow.

Quick as light after Jerry had boarded we had set the canvas. That day Jerry was the tea boy, as Vi took the wheel and I tended the foresail as we stretched away down river with the wind right bang on the nose. We were some little time slogging down to Erith and there Jerry decided we would call it a day. The wind was still from the north-east and that was a non-starter as far as our trip was concerned. Jerry told me that Vi would be coming for the whole trip with us, so at least we would be sure of good grub!

The weather wasn't very kind to us and I was to have nearly eight days lying at Erith before the weather showed any sign of moderating. The wind showed a swing to the south-west, and Jerry seemed to sense the shift and appeared on the jetty with his usual hail. As soon as he and Vi were on board, it was up barge boat in the davits and get our spread of canvas set. When we were head down the river we got the bowsprit lowered and gave her the jib.

We did well until we got down to Margate when the wind seemed to freshen. Jerry decided that we would anchor in Margate Roads. Out came my fishing gear with very good results and the fish were soon hanging in the rigging. Vi put some in the pan and they certainly tasted great. We washed them down with a couple of mugs of tea each and were able to end the day full and contented. A couple more days went by before the wind eased. It went even further to the west, so we had no problems going round the North Foreland. As we got further on so the sea size really increased. With a very long swell the poor old 'Smeed' was making heavy weather of it. We had only a couple of miles to go to bring Ramsgate abeam. Jerry was calling the old girl everything that he shouldn't. For all that, I was the one who was getting wet as I tended the headsails.

At last the welcome order came to drop the bowsprit jib and harbour stow the bowsprit. Our jib was always kept furled on the bowsprit and I think I was under the water most of the time whilst I got the gaskets around it. Although it seemed a long time, I wasn't out there a minute longer than was necessary.

As I got back inboard, Jerry was shouting for me to get aft. We hadn't seen the local huffler, and Jerry said he thought it would be too rough for him to come out. That meant we would have to go in without him.

Ivan's barge in a gentle breeze; the *George Smeed*, deep laden with all her cargo under her hatches.

Jerry had stood on a good half a mile or so past the piers and everything was made ready. As Jerry put us about so the *'Smeed'* filled herself level with all her rails and the run up to the pier was a very wet one. We were certainly moving fast and we had the topsail in and stowed as we took the piers. I noticed the huffler was on the west pier shouting at Jerry who had just slipped past me and gone to the foresail halyard. I was heaving like crazy at the main brails to stow as much of the mainsail as possible to try to slow the bugger up. Suddenly Jerry threw the halyards off the foresail with a shout aft to Vi. She promptly came hard around into the wind and Jerry then gave the barge a good scope of chain to bring us up. We were safe. Between us we gave her a good harbour stow, and then slowly hove her the long haul alongside the berth, getting the anchor as we came head to it. Vi had showed a great coolness in handling the barge, and I'm sure our job would have been a great deal more difficult without her.

Lying there a couple of days gave me thoughts once more of going into power, for I had been keeping a tally of the average earnings that we bargemen were getting. It made me realise that we were very poorly paid for our efforts. Learning that the expenses at Ramsgate were about the highest anywhere set me really thinking, especially when we had to lie with no money coming in.

Our orders from Ramsgate turned out to be for London empty to load grain back to Felixstowe. As we went round to the Thames we had a very bad trip. Coupled with my other concerns, it convinced me that I should pack it in, so as we passed Gravesend I strolled aft and gave Jerry a trip's notice. I think he had half been expecting me to go, although he kept saying, 'You won't learn much if you go into power.' I felt he was probably right, but I had to learn for myself.

After the barge had spent a tide at Erith Jerry gave me his usual shout and I went ashore for him. That's when I met the new mate. He was going to come on the trip down to Felixstowe, once we had loaded the *George Smeed,* as he hadn't been aboard a barge before. My thoughts were certainly with Jerry.

76 Lounging about at home for a few days, and having made quite a few phone calls there didn't seem to be a lot doing. It was with some surprise one day, as I strolled along the quay and bumped into my old schoolmate 'Tintack', to learn that he was going along to sign on aboard a small coaster as an ordinary seaman. He said he thought that they wanted a couple of ABs[1], so I strolled along with him to see if I could get a start. The walk proved lucky for I got signed on EDH[2], as I was not old enough to have gained the experience to rank AB. The work was the same, except I would be paid about ten bob (50p) a week less.

The other AB was another old friend of ours, so we only had to get to know the other lad and all would be well. He turned out to be the son of a university don and had been thrown out of his home. He was quite a lad and when he went ashore with his old Spanish guitar and he would wear the most ragged gear that he could find. He was nearly always drunk without having to buy any of his beer, as he was very talented musically.

Our time aboard was to be very short-lived. The Master was Irish and had his wife with him all the time. They were always having rows and the old bastard tried to take it out on us, so she was a far from happy ship.

After we had about nine weeks together we went to Blyth in Northumberland to load a cargo of coal for Par in Cornwall. In Blyth the clever 'Spanish Guitar' decided that he was going, so after his twenty-four hours' notice was up, off he went. The Master told us he would be sailing short-handed. When we asked about short-handed money he said that they wouldn't be paying it. We then involved the union and they told us we had the right to refuse to sail until we had an agreement with the Master. We moved the ship into the lay-by dock where she was to lie until there was an agreement worked out between the Master and the union. It was agreed that our watches would be two on and four off and we would be paid the short-handed money whilst we were at sea, and so we sailed.

The run south was not a very happy one. Whilst we were at Par it was pay day and the bugger tried to short change us. We all had a good moan and so he relented and paid us in full. From Par we had a short run across to Fowey and there we loaded a cargo of china clay for London. We spent a day loading, and had a swim, before battening down and pulling away as we lowered the derricks and rigged hoses for a good clean up.

I thought that the passage to London was going to be about time enough to serve out my notice, so I told the Master I had had enough. 'Tintack' and

[1] AB - Able Bodied Seaman. Qualified seaman with four years service since award of Efficient Deck Hand Certificate. [2] EDH - Efficient Deck Hand qualification awarded by the Board of Trade.

'Curly', the other AB also gave notice at the same time. The old man went loopy. Still he had to accept it and we left as soon as we could after our arrival at the Empire Paper Mills at Greenhithe, 'Tintack' and I going home to Ipswich and 'Curly' going down to Grays to see if he could pick something up. He turned out to be the lucky one of the three of us.

After being home a few days, time again turned out to be a bit of a drag and there didn't seem to be very much doing around the quay. I decided to pack a bag and go elsewhere, shipping aboard the *Reliance* to work my passage to London, and indeed for a few more days after we got there whilst they waited for orders.

Her Skipper, 'Young Spero'[1] used to like lying at Grays. I don't really know why, I think possibly there was a better selection of young ladies there for the lads to choose from.

Horlock's *Reliance*, loaded to her iron band, in the Wallet off the Essex resort of Clacton.

I was very unfortunate to lose a berth there by about half an hour. A small ship belonging to Goldsmiths wanted a mate, but by the time I found the Skipper in the pub the berth had just been taken. He told me that another of

[1] 'Young Spero' - Derek Ling, son of 'Spero', who was also known as 'Old Spero' to differentiate between father and son.

their craft wanted a second engineer so I popped along to their office. They sent me back to the pub, the Theobald's Arms, where I met Swiney, the Master, and Jock, the Engineer. After several questions from Jock they decided to give me the job, despite me telling them that the only engineering I had done was to replace a cycle chain, the little I'd learnt from the *Lady Jean*, and to make a one-valve radio at school.

Runic was a big old ex-sailing barge and, like a few of Goldsmiths other craft, had been converted to power to keep pace with the Dutch craft that were taking over and getting all the short haul work. Our freight rates were kept low to compete with them, so our wages were likewise kept down. However, for five pounds a week and a couple of pounds more in cargo bonus, I considered I was well off, especially as we were even paid when the hold was empty. It was a better deal than we all had as sailormen.

Our engines were Bolinders, of the hot bulb variety, and were always giving us trouble, so Jock was always diving inside them. I got to know all about hot bulbs, injectors and con-rods, all the things that caused our problems. Our longest runs in the *Runic* were from Blyth in Northumberland to the Isle of Wight, right up to Newport. Our top speed was only about four knots so passages could be long.

If the weather was bad Jock and I would be battened down in the engine room for a couple of days at a time. Food used to come down the vent on top of the engine room. The telegraph would ring and, regardless of the ship diving about and rolling, down would come the dixie full of soup or tea and sandwiches. Jock or I would spend a couple of hours each off-watch, lying on an old, oil-saturated mattress between the engines. Most of the Bolinder engines were very demanding of attention whilst running, with regular oiling needed. There was no way we could both drop off to sleep or the engines would have seized up.

Being a weekly servant in the *Runic* it was my duty to give the Master a week's notice should I want to pack up, so as we loaded a cargo in Blyth I gave Swiney my notice. He kept saying, 'Where are you going?' thinking I had been poached. But all I could say was, 'Don't know yet.' Swiney thought I had been offered a berth, and the skippers didn't like that sort of thing going on unless it was to their advantage. Any rate, Swiney had to accept my notice, and I thought that with our normal run we would be back somewhere in the London river by the time my notice was worked out.

I had been in the *Runic* for nearly six months. I had learnt quite a lot in that time, for when the weather was reasonable or we were empty I spent plenty of time in the wheelhouse poring over the charts. Swiney liked to explain them to me and used to say, 'You would rather be on the bridge, wouldn't you?' and I had to agree with him. I then told him I wanted to go for my ticket as soon as I was around the twenty mark. He thought that with the way the work was going that was the best thing that I could do.

Our trip going south was in bad weather and I think that the *Runic* was trying to tell me something. Jock and I had spent most of the time down in the engine room except for a short spell when we had gone through the Downs. Swiney made to run into Dover, but changed his mind when we got down off there and decided to keep plodding along westward. Getting down to Beachy Head took a long time and Swiney decided that we should go into Newhaven and have a few hours out of the foul weather. It was really blowing and there was one hell of a sea running. As Swiney turned the old girl from Beachy Head towards Newhaven she really decided to let us know that she could roll with the wind and weather on the port bow.

The *Runic* was just filling herself all the way up to the top of her rails and before she was able to clear, the next lot had rolled aboard. We didn't need anything to go wrong now for we were fast approaching a lee shore with a harbour that was not easy to take in a craft like the *Runic*. It was a great relief when we got into the lee of the western breakwater and then found a berth on the quay not too far from the pub. Our Master knew where to go!

Once we had got inside the harbour the most sensible thing to do would have been to get scrubbed up and turn in. But no, not us lot! It was scrub up, have a bit of a nosh up, and then go ashore for a beer. Our few hours there were to run into a couple of days before there was any sign of improvement in the weather. Eventually Swiney decided that it was time for us to go, but it was about nine o'clock in the evening, and we still had a couple of hours boozing to get in. It didn't take a lot for us to persuade Swiney to stay a bit longer.

By the time we got back on board, Curly and I just turned in, incapable of doing anything. So it was Jock and Swiney who let go and took her out on their own.

As we neared the Nab Tower to the east of the island I sort of came to and didn't take long to get into my stride. The tea and bacon and eggs were soon going, for on board here anybody would do the cooking. Curly and I got our breakfast and then I fried breakfast for Jock and Swiney and all the sore heads seemed to disappear. Although Swiney and Jock had stood a long watch, nothing was said to cause any arguments. Soon we closed Cowes Roads and that's where Curly and I got the old girl ready for discharge.

When we got towards the top of the river my place was in the engine room, working the port engine. Jock always said that the starboard one used to want to stop more than start. As we manoeuvred, the engines lost heat and this made them want to stop. With a few belts ahead and astern we soon got alongside, and then would come the telegraph ring, 'Finished with engines.' It would take Jock and me about an hour to clean up the engine room and get things ready for the next trip.

After our discharge at Newport, 'Curly' and I were soon busy getting the hold ready to load stone from the Berry Head Quarry to take to London. The

The bulky *Runic* had her bow rails raised when converted to full power. Some comedian had a point to make about the competence of those on board, an 'L' plate stuck to her stem.

hold was checked before any cargo was put in so we really had to make a good job of it. Swiney wanted to get as much of the west-going tide as possible so once the water was around us we cast off before we had really floated. Just as we lifted Swiney rang down, 'Full speed ahead' and she churned her way off for my last trip aboard.

Out through the Needles was easy going and so it was across Lyme Bay. If we had too much swell when empty, or bad head winds, the old girl would have had to lie windbound. We were no good in any sort of a seaway as the props just flayed the air.

Alongside the jetty at Berry Head it only took about twenty minutes for us to load. We were all involved in battening down and getting ready for sea. Then it was into Brixham to fill up our bunkers. They had nobody else coming on the berth for a few hours, so Swiney decided that he would lie there until we had an east going tide.

As we rolled our way to the east, what a smashing run we had. It was beautifully clear and calm weather all the way up the Channel and on up to Grays. After we had anchored, Swiney was able to nip off home, telling us he wanted to be picked up on the low water next day, ready for our run up to Nacovia Wharf at Fulham. We were able to go ashore for a couple of pints in the evening. I was keeping my ears to the ground at this time but there were no mate's berths to be had locally. I had been assured by the gent in the office that I was next in line, but as I hadn't heard anything, I guessed I would have to look elsewhere after we came back down from Fulham.

We had a good run up, a quick discharge at Fulham and an easy return to Grays. After lying for a couple of days there, without any news for me, Swiney suggested I gave Everards a ring. As he was not leaving for Ipswich, to load scrap iron for Middlesborough, for at least a couple of days, I decided to leave it one more day before I would give Everards a call.

My phone call across the river was to a Mr Kimber who was the shore-based shipping manager. After a couple of attempts I managed to get hold of him. He said, 'When can you start?' and I told him I was free to start straight away, but what was he offering? He did not reply directly but said, 'Bring your gear. I'll send 'Brusher' in the trot boat over to pick you up.' In about half an hour the motor boat pulled alongside the *Runic* and I took my departure with a cheery wave to the lads and was gone. That's how I came to meet old 'Brusher', and to strike up a friendship that was to last quite a few years.

I was directed to Mr Kimber's office and spent a good hour with him. He went right through what I'd done and also what I wanted to do. He not only offered me a job I was prepared to accept, but also gave me a lot of sound advice as to what could be in the none too distant future. The conversation went on until it was established that I could go AB in one of the ships, or as mate of one of their small barges, the *Lady Mary*, or mate of the large steel barge, the

Greenhithe. I couldn't believe my ears when he said that, for that was exactly the way I wanted to go. When I asked about the Master seeing me, he just said that it would be all right, and it appears that was the way that the firm worked. Mr Kimber could start who he liked on any craft as could any of the Masters or a shipping superintendent, and that's the way they

Everard's *Lady Mary* in the London river.

made sure that they could keep crew spaces filled, and that's how I came to be the mate of the *Greenhithe*.

Getting aboard the barge was the next step. I rang Bob Roberts, her Master, and he told me to pick up the keys from the watchman at the yard gate. He said to ask 'Brusher' to run me off afloat, and then went on to tell me where the mate and the third hand, if we could find one, lived for'ard in the fo'c'sle. He said that he would see me next morning. He didn't think there would be much in the way of cargoes about, but if I got some of the gear working easy he would make sure that I got yard pay for doing it and so not be starving!

After boarding and dumping my gear for'ard I went back on deck to take stock of my surroundings. The main thing that I noticed was that everything was covered in a heavy blanket of white cement dust. That meant I had plenty to do, so I set to with a will to sort some order out of it all. Having no third hand at that time meant I was on my own, for Bob lived at Bexleyheath and spent most of his time at home.

A large part of my preparatory work was using the oil can and the grease pot, and I certainly used plenty of it over those first few days whilst we were waiting for orders. Bob came aboard and we had a chat. He seemed to like what I was doing. I had borrowed the steam hose from the tank cleaning barge that we were lying alongside and our decks and coamings were all as clean as new pins. To get really aloft I set the topsail. What a job that proved to be, but I did manage it and then I could climb the hoops of the topsail from the head of the mainmast. I took the chance to get a new house flag from the stores, climbed to the very top of the topmast, cut the old flag out of the frame and sewed in the new one. Then I did the horrible job of greasing the spar from top to bottom. Plenty of oil was put into the blocks at the top of the topmast which take the halyards for the topsail and the staysail. At last things were beginning to work a little better.

Bob came aboard after I had just come down from aloft. As the topsail was still set he could see what I had been up to; the new flag and the greasing up. He started to give me a rollicking for going up off the deck like that without somebody else being on board. I didn't take a lot of notice of him and he could see that, and it was soon forgotten.

I passed the comment that it seemed a hell of a long way down to the deck. Bob then told me that we had the *Alf Everard's* gear in. She was a three hundred ton barge, against our one hundred and eighty tons, so we had plenty more gear than we really needed, as I was to find out later.

Bob also told me to expect the *Greenhithe* to be just as cranky as the *George Smeed*, but was very unlikely to carry any top gear away. After a few more days of general chores and getting the hold cleaned up, Bob said that our new mizzen gaff and sail were ready, and before long it was all set up and we could say we were ready and fit to load. I had been mate of the *Greenhithe* for just over two weeks.

Having said to myself that at long last I had got myself into the right company, I soon began to look a little more closely at my future. Bob had told me that the firm would always transfer a bargeman into a motor ship if that was what they wanted, and several bargemen had done just that. It seemed that the options I sought would be available to me.

The *Greenhithe* looked a massive barge as one looked at her from a distance. She had a very big sheer, both for'ard and aft, and also a big whaleback wheelhouse all adding to the impression of size. I was to learn that she was a good craft, reasonably dry when running before heavy weather and also when punching into it, but when beam on she had to be one of the wettest. The waist would fill up and the old bugger wouldn't recover unless we got sail off her.

Our orders came at last, and what a pain they turned out to be. We had to pop across the river to the Tunnel cement works and there take on a full cargo of cement, a couple of hundred tons, to be taken to a ship lying in the Royal Albert Dock.

I soon found out that the *Greenhithe* was a very heavy vessel to work, more so than anything I had been in to date. To heave her topsail up on one's own was a major task and the deck work would leave you knackered. As the *Greenhithe* did not carry a dolly wire, when manoeuvring in the dock I had to scull a line away, get back aboard and then Bob or I would heave on the mastcase winch to move the barge to our berth. It made for very hard work.

She also had ship style hatches, the hold beams went fore and aft and the hatches went from coaming to beam athwart[1] the barge. That meant you had twice as many as a normal barge. Also, ours were two inches thick and very heavy, so there was a great deal of effort required when opening and closing them.

Bob was nearly always at home at Bexleyheath whilst we were in the London area, but wherever we were I always seemed to be kept very busy. I soon gained confidence in the dock and deck work through being left on my own most of the time. On that first occasion, soon after discharging the cargo, I was busy sweeping the hold out when Bob jumped aboard and said, 'Don't bother, mate, we're going back for more cement.' We were going to load at Bevens Wharf at Greenhithe for the Royal Albert Dock again.

Then began the struggle to get down and out of the dock. It was always full of lighters and the blasted things were nearly always adrift. When we did get a line on them we just seemed to heave the bloody things towards us, which

[1] At 90° to the centre line of a vessel - across the width of the craft.

meant a lot of frustration. Still, that was all part of the game. Once we were clear of the lock and had our spread of canvas aloft, docks were forgotten until the next time.

The short run from the docks to Greenhithe was soon done, and we even managed to save our tide on to our berth at Bevens Wharf ready to load. As we slept we were being loaded. The night-shift lads here were very good for they even put the beams in and the hatches on. Being heavily loaded we would be a long time floating. They made sure that as soon as we did float we could get away, to allow another craft on to the berth. They worked well for their beer money and deserved the five shillings (25p.) we gave them.

It was a short sail up to the Albert Dock as we had a good fair wind. Once again, after we had entered the dock and found our ship, Bob was away home. We were to lie sometime with this cargo and we had a lot more demurrage to come than freight money when at last we did get rid of it. A good thing about the *Greenhithe* that pleased me was that she was a very dry barge and no pumping was required. Lying alongside us in the dock was the *Lady Mary*, one of the craft Mr Kimber had spoken to me about, and they seemed to have to pump all day so I was glad I stayed away from that one!

The crew of the barge ahead of us, which should have been unloaded before us, were on their way home to Rochester so the ship worker pushed us in before them. Next morning the air turned a funny colour as the other Skipper arrived back and went for the ship worker. Apparently he had told the Skipper he wouldn't be needed. Despite the row, he just had to wait until we were empty and had been pulled clear.

I had rung Bob the evening before so he was aboard nice and early in the morning. 'Don't sweep the hold out,' he said 'we are going back to Tunnel Cement.' That time we would be going to Colchester for discharge. As Colchester was considered an import dock we could still ignore our load line. After we had loaded and cleared the Tunnel works it was everything set, and that meant the lot, including two jibs on the bowsprit. It made a fine sight to anyone who was away from us. To us it meant plenty of hard work but at the same time it was a great feeling to belong to this crew.

The trip to Colchester went along as smoothly as we could have hoped. Towing up the last bit from Marriages Bight gave me plenty of time to get ready for discharge as well as to look about. The River Colne is quite a pretty river as it goes into the upper reaches. The little motorboat had got us up to the quay in good time, so we were able to swing in order to get away that much earlier once we had discharged. But emptying the holds of cement was not an option in the pouring rain that day.

Bob was away up to the agent's soon after we got alongside. After he came back with my mail and sub, he told me that we would have to make a good job of the hold as we were going to Ipswich to load a cargo of sugar for

The powerfully built and rigged *Greenhithe* was constructed by Fellowes at Great Yarmouth in 1923.

London. After we had been at Colchester for a couple of days the weather improved enabling the cargo to be discharged, but Bob had an enforced stay at home for another couple of days as the weather turned really bad the moment we were emptied.

Even when we left our little tug was having difficulty pulling us through Marriage's Bight, as he had all the way down from Colchester. The wind was very strong from the south-east, and I had by then got the bowsprit down and the topsail and mainsail were already set. As soon as we had cleared Freshwater jetty, Bob gave the order to cast off the tug, the *Greenhithe's* sails filled, and we were off. Soon we were doing long and short boards to get out of the Colne.

I had got the anchor on the bow, set up the bobstay and, when the chance came, I nipped out along the bowsprit, flung off the gaskets and soon had the jib set. We were then able to set the mizzen and so the old girl was really put through her paces.

Once we had cleared the Colne and we were able to look our course down the Wallet, the *Greenhithe* showed that she certainly could go. Bob said she was on her best point of sailing and although it seemed we were almost lying on our beam ends she was steering like a yacht, and gave me a very exhilarating sail. Passing through Harwich, Bob said to stow the jib. As I dropped it down and nipped out along the bowsprit and got my harbour stow, so Bob got the barge balanced again by stowing the mizzen. By the time I had stowed up and got the bowsprit hove up, we were rounding Collimer Point.

There we met a few more craft making their way up to Ipswich, some empty and some loaded. Bob reckoned the empty ones could well be going after sugar, and that's when he told me that we had a priority to load as it was Everard's own contract.

As the wind stayed in the south-east we had been blessed with a fair wind all the way up the river and had moored alongside another of our fleet, the *Veronica*, to await our lock-in turn. The *Veronica's* Skipper, Jack Nunn, gave us his turn also, so as soon as we were tied alongside the *Scotsman* we made ready to load.

Whilst we were loading the next day one of the local lads

Everard's *Veronica*, retired from cargo carrying, was kept for racing, becoming arguably the most successful barge to compete during the first hundred years of the Thames Sailing Barge Match..

came around to ask for the third hand's job. He had been in a couple of local craft, was quite a wiry type and he suited us just fine. Jim was to make a big difference to our crew and he certainly eased the workload.

After we finished loading and had got all squared up, Jim and I got us down to the pier head by heaving and running our line away, as the wind was still blowing very hard from the south-east. Bob jumped aboard and said the motorboat would be coming into the dock to get hold of us and pull us away clear.

Whilst we lay waiting for the outward lock, Bob had told me that once we got down beyond Harwich we would probably take a long board out beyond the north-east Gunfleet buoy, on a very reduced amount of sail if it stayed blowing like it was. Then we would make one board back and see how the time was and also the run of tide, and then make up our minds as to what we would do next. Bob had got it well worked out for by the time we were at the north-east Gunfleet we were, to put it into Bob's words, 'gilling along', as we just had the mainsail set to the sprit, topsail rucked, foresail, mizzen and the jib on the bowsprit.

Once we had passed the Gunfleet, Bob kept us standing on seaward. How far we stood I couldn't say, but I do know that we were going along quite comfortably. When at last Bob swung us round onto the port tack, to shape back and up into the Swin, we really put plenty of water across our midships, but we were soon round and making very good progress in the right direction.

I could see why quite a few craft had anchored at Shotley, for out there in the dark, with the wind roaring in the rigging and the sea rising quite fast as the young flood made in, looking out from the *Greenhithe's* wheelhouse all one could see was white water. Talking to Bob, he explained that if you kept the craft going easy the tide would do the work, and being steel hulled we didn't have to worry about pumping.

As we passed the Shoebury buoy Bob said, 'Right lads, let's give her all the mainsail!' and the old girl picked up well with just this extra bit of sail. Passing through Gravesend Reach, up went the topsail. We had made quite good time and, after our arrival at Tate and Lyle at Silvertown, we again had the privilege of taking priority.

A quick discharge meant that Bob never had time to pop home that trip, for we had orders that would take us straight back to Ipswich. About three hours after our arrival we were only waiting for Jim to come back aboard with the shopping and then we were ready for the off.

The run down was pretty routine, a few slams and bangs and the wind still lying in the south-east, so we made a good trip of it. I was very surprised as we passed through Shotley to see some of the other craft that had left Ipswich Dock with us, still lying there. Bob explained that that was why Everards had the clause put in about their fleet taking priority, because we were prepared to get on with the job. The arrangement only really applied to the *Will Everard* or us in the *Greenhithe*, for we were way out of the class and shape of the rest so we really could have a go[1].

After we arrived and loaded at Ipswich we were soon on the way back to the London River again. Much to our disgust, we were dogged by very fickle winds, a complete contrast to the previous trip. Still, we arrived quite some time ahead of the barges that had loaded with us on the first of these two trips, so I really had quite a few pounds in the old wallet. That was something very new to me and Jimmy, and we had a few more pints than we should have had.

The *Greenhithe* laden, with bowsprit up, 'staysail rigged' in the confines of the river.

[1] *Will Everard* and *Greenhithe* could be pressed harder than most of the other, much older, wooden craft.

90 Our next orders were for close by Silvertown, and as soon as we had the last of the sugar discharged we only had a quick trip to Woolwich Reach, there to enter the basin for the King George Dock. That gave us a very long haul up through the Albert Dock to reach the Victoria Dock. We were loading out of the mill so we didn't have any delays. Until we were about half loaded we didn't know our port of discharge, and then the foreman came and told me that we were bound to Reeds of Norwich. I said to Jim that it was a new one on me and he said that he had also never been there, so we both looked forward to the run with great anticipation.

I suggested an early start next day, so whilst Jim went out to the shops, I gave the old girl a good scrub round. After we had got tea over, Jim and I went and had a couple of beers, then it was early back and turn in. We meant to get an early start the next day and were having a nice cup of tea at five thirty. As the toshers went down just after six it was my intention to try for a pull down the dock. The third one away was my lucky one as he pulled us down for a quarter of tea.

By seven-fifteen we were in a good position to lock out, but as they did a shift change about eight it would be nearer nine before they were ready for us. It always seemed that they would lock craft in first and make more congestion; still we got out and got a turn on the pier head to await Bob's arrival. After a few more teas, Bob jumped aboard about eleven o'clock with his usual 'Let's go lads!' And so we were outward bound once again. It was Bob's intention to stop at Greenhithe overnight and let us store up the next morning.

The firm did us proud for stores. They supplied everything except food, so we were certainly much better off than most barge crews. The local shop also provided us with generous helpings, the price of a pound of sugar usually getting us nearer a pound and a half. Up until this time Bob was still grubbing himself, mainly because he was hardly ever on board. He used to survive on a pair of kippers followed by hunks of bread and jam, and ale when he had the chance. We had noticed, however, that when Jim made the old duff, Bob was always in for a helping. On the second day of any trip, when we always used to fry the remainder and then put a nice generous helping of syrup over it, Bob joined in and agreed that nothing could taste better.

For flour we got plenty from the hold sweepings from some craft or another. The London dockers always made sure there were plenty of spillages when they had dried fruit to unload. Many sailorman had a carrier bag of something dropped on the deck whilst waiting at a ship or just lying alongside a lighter overnight. Looking under the corner of a hatch cover, one never knew what to expect. Lightermen never seemed to put hatch boards on unless they had loaded bonded materials.

Once we had taken on board our stores, as far as Jim and I were concerned, we were ready for the off. We had even lowered the bowsprit for I knew that Bob would want the jib set as soon as he got the barge head down the river. I suggested to Jim that we should have a pint while we waited for Bob, and he was in full agreement. We nipped into The Pier pub and found Bob was there for a quick one before us, so our pint turned into a couple or so! About one o'clock, it being high water, Bob said, 'Right lads, let's go.' Soon we were back on board and away with everything set. Yes, the lot was bent on her including the two jibs on the bowsprit. With full sail, a fair tide and the wind out from the south-east we couldn't have had conditions any better. Later on as the day turned to early evening and we were still carrying the same sail, Bob suggested that I get a couple of hours' sleep.

Our arrangement at sea was that I slept on the locker down in the main cabin aft. One long continuous banging meant get up on deck as fast as you can, just a couple of bangs meant the change the watch. This system seemed to work very well. Bob had sent the boy Jim below after he had made the evening cocoa for him. Jim did have a couple of hours at the wheel earlier,but if the night was fine it was always Bob's way to send the third hand below for the night.

The double bang came for me around nine-thirty, so I turned and rolled myself off the locker. I put the kettle on, and just poked my head outside the cabin hatch to let Bob know that I was about. The kettle was soon on the boil and I took myself and my mug of cocoa into the shelter of our whaleback[1]. As I was by then fully awake Bob told me our position and course and said to call him if anything changed. I was left to a lonely deck, and although the stars were all out, the night was very dark. Looking under our lee I could see the glow of Harwich. My thoughts wandered to those lights, and what was going on amongst them in the pubs and houses.

After running some time on Bob's course some sixth sense told me something was not quite right and so I took a much better look under our lee. What a shock. If I didn't haul out quite a bit we were not going to clear the Rough Towers. I put it down to my daydreaming, so I gave myself a rollicking and was always more vigilant afterwards.

Around half past midnight Bob, without a call from me, put his head out of the hatch and asked how we were doing. I told him we were doing okay, but he didn't really need me to tell him because by looking under the mainsail he had seen all the landmarks that he needed to see.

Bob always had a little yarn of some sort to tell, and it was on the change of the watch that he used to give you one. It was at times like that that I realised

[1] A whaleback was the distinctive open-fronted (usually) wheelhouse on a sailing barge, and other sailing vessels, so-called after the distinctive curve of the after end of its roof.

I was very lucky to be in this type of craft, and especially with a Skipper like Bob. He oozed confidence and had the power of passing this on, so I gradually found I was able to cope with the watch and began to take things in my stride.

I had awoken to the wonderful smell of bacon cooking, and there was our Jim over the stove getting Bob's breakfast. My mug of tea was ready so I could relieve Bob at the wheel. By the time he had eaten his breakfast Jim had had his too. Jim then relieved me at the wheel and I got mine. Bob was able to go below for a rest whilst we were sailing ever nearer Yarmouth, the entrance to the River Yare and 'Broadland'. Finally the pier heads came into view and the tug was shortly to be seen coming for us. Bob said we could have sailed in, but we would take the tug. If we didn't, when we really wanted him, he wouldn't appear.

It was then time to stow the two jibs and get the bowsprit up. Jim and I were both refreshed with a good kip and a great breakfast, so our work that morning seemed to go very well. Feeding our towrope out to the tug was, we knew, going to be a lot easier than pulling it in. To my surprise, we shortened up after we had got round Brush Quay, so we were then only a few yards behind the tug. Bob told me that the same tug would be pulling us through the town bridge ready for the Norwich tug to pull us away next day.

So that night we spent lying near the Vauxhall Bridge at the top of the harbour. We were against the quay before the tug eased back alongside, so we could pull the towrope in quite easily. A few beers and an early night were called for.

Our destination was still a long tow away, but the next morning the Norwich tug was with us bright and early. Being my first trip up that river, my eyes were all about. Standing forward and listening to the old plod of the steam tug and the swishing of the water running past our bow had a very special sound of its own. The river birds were also well about and didn't seem to be disturbed by the vast hull of the *Greenhithe* as she slipped along. As soon as the water had closed under our stern the birds were landing, picking at grubs no doubt stirred up by our passage. At all the little places that we passed through we were greeted by friendly waves, and all too soon for me our journey was at its end. After passing through the last of the bridges we were soon slowing to take the wharf.

The up-river tug, the *Mustard Pot* seen in Gt. Yarmouth, belonged to the Norwich mustard makers, Colmans.

Once we had moored up, the foreman came out and said they wouldn't be starting us until the next morning, so Bob knew that we would have a couple of days there and promptly said that he would get his train home. Jim and I didn't like the berth at Reeds, for we were right opposite a very busy road and the noise was a lot more than we were used to, but in the evening, after a few beers, we had no trouble getting off to sleep.

At the end of our first day discharging we had about three-quarters of the cargo out and we were due to finish around two o'clock the next day. The tug was ordered for that time, so we just hoped that things would go to plan. The next day started well and just after midday the last of our cargo was being swept into the elevator. Bob jumped aboard saying that we had no orders and that we were to ring when we got back to Yarmouth.

The river tug came popping through the bridge, so on went the tow rope and we were away with a nice fine day and a good ebb tide, soon slipping along behind the tug with our next freight still a mystery.

At Reedham railway bridge we seemed to meet some delay and the tug had to round us up head to tide. Apparently we stopped on instructions from our firm's office. We were given orders to go alongside the sugar works at Cantley. Bob couldn't believe it. We were going to load sugar for Bridlington, in Yorkshire, he said. The pub at Cantley, the Red House, was only a couple of hundred yards away from our berth so we didn't have far to go for a pint. Bob, with his old squeeze box, kept the few people that were in the pub alive for the evening!

Loading at Cantley didn't take very long and Bob was keen to get away as we were in the middle of high pressure weather. The wind from the south-west would suit us just fine. Our old friend, the small tug, didn't keep us waiting at all for as Bob was signing up, Jim and I sorted the towing gear out, and as Bob stepped back aboard we let go the slip ropes and were away. Bob had also signed the tug's paperwork so we could tow down near the pier heads before we let him go.

The little tug was not allowed outside the harbour, but Bob said we had a very strong ebb tide and with everything sheeted hard in we should have no trouble clearing the piers. And so it was. As we went round the corner of Brush Quay the old girl picked up the stiff south-west breeze. Soon after, it was, 'Let go the tug!' and as soon as Jim and I had hauled the tow rope in we were jumping about to set up the bowsprit and get the jibs on her. Having cleared up and got the final lashings all settled we were soon back into our seagoing routine.

Bob chose to give me the first watch, which I was pleased to get, for I had a few buoys to steer on, and this made knowing where I was so much easier. All too soon we had passed through the North Cockle gateway and then it was back on the compass.

We were certainly cracking along with a good breeze, and whilst it kept up we were in with a chance of a good passage. My four hours on watch flew by. As the old girl was more or less looking after herself I decided I would let Bob sleep on. It was to be another hour and a half before he came on deck, saying how refreshed he felt. Jim was preparing a nice meal which was due in about half an hour, so by the time we had sunk a mug of tea, Bob and I were able to go below to eat.

Jim had the watch until Bob relieved him for his meal and I climbed onto the locker and was soon fast asleep. For my next watch the breeze from the west was still with us and was about a force four. I came up to a very dark night, but our route was well lit by the light vessels around the Humber. Bob reeled out which was what and it soon unfolded to me, as I had studied the chart before taking over the watch. The wind remained good for us and Bob said that if it kept up until we passed the tide setting us into the Humber, we would soon be there. He would then tell me what the drill was for us, as there were no tugs or any other help for going in to Bridlington.

Bob was able to have his time below in comfort, but the wind had fallen away quite a bit when it was time for him to take over. The visibility had also taken a tumble. I had obtained a reasonable fix before the visibility closed in. After a couple of hours of Bob's watch the wind had fallen further, but the visibility was about the same. Based on our soundings, Bob decided we would bring up as he reckoned we should be somewhere close to the entrance. As the wind was touching off the land we had no worries about going to anchor.

Early dawn came in, the fog was blowing clear and the wind, which was very light, had backed into the south. The lights ashore started to show through the murk, and amongst them Bob was able to pick out the pier end light. After a couple more hours outside on our anchor Bob said, 'Let's go for it.'

First he gave us a brief rundown as to what was likely to happen. As

The narrow entrance to Bridlington Harbour, where the discharging berths were alongside the harbour wall seen bottom left. The pleasure steamer *Yorkshireman* restricts the entrance on the right.

there was no tug we might get asked by a fisherman if we wanted a tow, but we had to make sure of the price before we gave them a rope. He said if that didn't happen we would sail into the entrance, down our headsail, and shoot the old girl up into the berth, which sort of lay into the south-east. It would probably be down anchor and run lines off ashore in the boat if we got it wrong.

Bob made a very good fetch into the harbour, and by dropping the foresail we were able to shoot up alongside one of our firm's small coasters that was lying alongside. It had discharged sugar and was waiting for water out. We ran aground about halfway along his side, which was the usual way to stop a barge if one was in sheltered water. Stowing up didn't take Jim and me long and so we were soon ready for our discharge. When the wharf foreman arrived about eight-thirty, he told us that we wouldn't be starting until the next day as we had not informed him of our arrival. Suitably equipped craft were able to send an ETA[1] over their ship's radio. Bob was cursing all day, as it was perfect weather for unloading. He spent most of the day pounding on his typewriter, so some good came out of it.

Next morning we started to discharge. We were covering up and uncovering most of the day, for the wind had shifted to the south-east and freshened, and of course the rain had come in with it. Still, in a day and a half we had got it all clear. After we had swept the hold out and generally squared up Bob came back with orders for Keadby empty to load coal for the South. As it was still blowing quite hard it was clear there was no way we were going to get out that night, so we'd see what the next day brought.

It dawned with a very fresh wind, still from the south-east, and I couldn't see us getting away without some help. As I went ashore for the papers I kept my eyes open for any activity on the quayside, but there was none. I told Bob that I had looked for something going off but no joy. He said, 'I'll go and see the Harbour Master. He'll know if we are in with a chance.'

As we hadn't had breakfast, and were not afloat, we thought it best to have the old bacon and eggs whilst we had the chance. Afterwards, Bob and I took a walk ashore to the harbour office, but there was no sign of life. There were a couple of old fishermen sitting outside and Bob let them know what we wanted. They just laughed and said, 'Not whilst it's like this you won't get out.' Bob knew that without a tow there was no way we would be able to get offshore.

He couldn't solve it and so went below in disgust. I was full of hope but didn't know why. A trawler came inwards from the sea and he had to lie alongside us to take on water. Jim approached him about buying a bit of fish, which he was happy to sell us. Jim also told them about our predicament, and they said to tell our Skipper to give them a look. Our Jim promptly got Bob on deck and after quite a bit of haggling they agreed a figure of ten pounds to tow us out and three miles offshore. Bob moaned and said it was twice as much as he would like to pay, but we were in a bad spot and the fishermen knew it.

[1] Estimated time of arrival.

Going head to wind didn't take too long and the fisherman laughed as I passed the towrope over and said, 'Break that if you can.' They pulled us offshore as agreed, and we set up a sort of storm rig as the wind was very squally and there was quite a swell running. The run up to the Humber was quite something, and the old *Greenhithe* made very heavy weather of it. Being empty didn't help us at all. As we got clear of Spurn Point Bob said to keep the Bull Forts on the port bow. I was glad to have something to do.

To stand and just think what might happen is not good. We then squared away into the Humber; the tide was running out and there was one hell of a swell. The poor old girl was certainly doing plenty of yawing about but we were going in quite well. The wind was also steadily increasing but from the south-east and so as the tide eased we were really going well over the ground.

As we got into the Hull Roads, Bob said there was no way we were going to bring up. It was a fair wind right up to Keadby and the tide was turning in our favour. It was a hair-raising experience for Jim and me to be bounding along in the pitch dark. As we passed the humps of the Whitton Sands, Bob was explaining about the number of ships that had been rolled over through touching the bottom thereabouts, as the tide ran so very fast through there. Bob reassured us that with the amount of wind we had we would have no problems controlling *Greenhithe* that night and, laughing as he said it, as long as the steering didn't fail or the mast carry away!

Where the Trent and the Ouse split is another bad place. It has to be treated with great caution as one could easily get pushed into the wrong river, but that night Bob had the wind to control us. To stop when we got up to the Keadby jetty we stowed up and put our head on the shore. Our stern swung up and we fell alongside one of our ships, the *Apricity*.

The next day Bob told us that we were bound for Harwich. He said my share would be the princely sum of seventeen pounds. We had been doing very well of late and I had been earning money faster than I could spend it, getting richer all the time.

If we were loaded before the *Apricity* was ready to leave, Bob's old friend Tom, her Skipper, had offered us a tow down and, of course, at no cost. Bob and I would have a trip without any towage, which on the coal run could be quite expensive. Our luck was still holding for as soon as the *Apricity* was loaded, they just dropped up above the jetty with the tide. We dropped into the berth and within the space of half an hour or so were putting the hatches on. To think that we had loaded one hundred and sixty-eight tons all snug under the hatches so quickly. Our coal lockers had also been filled by the ever-busy Jim.

The towrope was passed to the Mate of the *Apricity* as they slid down alongside. He asked how we pulled it in and I said, 'With great difficulty.' Still, the tow was certainly going to make a difference to our pay packets. It began with the tide under us and we were off at a good rate. Bob had expected Tom

Everard's *Apricity* loaded first at Keadby, but waited for *Greenhithe* to load and gave her a tow down.

to let us go in Hull Roads but, being an old bargeman, he had decided to pull us as far off to windward as he could.

We were scooping the water over our bows as Tom got us past the Bull Forts, where he decided to let us go. He gave us a toot on his whistle and our towrope was cast off. As soon as it was back on board Jim and I flew about to get the bowsprit set up and the jib on it. Once that was done we were able to give the old girl all her basic sails. She seemed to come alive and was certainly a lot drier. As I got aft I said as much to Bob who responded by saying, 'Right, you might as well have her then.'

After Bob had stepped away from the wheel he gave me the order to hold her on the starboard tack as we needed to get offshore. The smell of kippers cooking wafted up through the hatch and that reminded me that I was hungry, but first I had a nice mug of tea. After Jim had enjoyed a bit of grub it was my turn, so he took the watch whilst I had my nosh.

Bob put his head up through the hatch after we had been standing offshore for about an hour and a half and said, 'Right, mate, shove us round.' Whilst Jim tended the head the old girl came round, with lots of noise as everything was slamming and banging. It wasn't long before we were filling away on the port tack and standing back towards the land. This kept us inside the Race Bank and eventually gave some lee from the mainland as we approached Cromer.

I had been sent below for a couple of hours' rest and must have fallen into a deep sleep for I was well away when the heavy slamming of Bob's boots made me wake with a start. It was the emergency call. As I got to my feet and jumped into my boots I could feel the old girl was lying on her beam ends. I knew that I had to get on deck fast.

Leaping through the hatchway I could see Bob was struggling with the wheel and he shouted to me to get the topsail off her. Whilst I had been below Bob had put us around again so that we were on the starboard tack. That meant that the topsail halyard I needed to reach on the brail winch on the port side of the mast would be under water. Once I had got to it, I held my breath and ducked into the water to get the handle. I quickly lifted the pawl on the winch and let the topsail come down with a run. The *Greenhithe* quickly responded by lifting her lee rails and deck out of the water. I pulled down the topsail clewlines and things became a lot quieter.

Back aft I stood in the shelter of the whaleback for a few minutes as another heavy squall passed through. When that cleared Bob said he was going to put us back on the port tack, and then get me to harbour stow the topsail. The barge swung through the wind with all the usual banging and crashing associated with heavy weather manoeuvres. Then it was up aloft for me, to get the gaskets around the flogging canvas. That was not the easiest job on a calm day, but it was a real challenge on a dirty night like that. Once it was done Bob got me to heave the mainsail in up to the sprit. Having made us trim and as much as we could, ready for anything, Bob said, 'Dry up a bit, mate, let's have a brew and you finish your watch below,' for which I was very thankful.

After what seemed like a good sleep I was again called to stand a watch. There was only about an hour to go before daylight and the dawning showed very grey and bleak, however, the sky had given us the hint of less wind. Our Jim was enjoying a spell at the wheel. We were going to let Bob have a lie in, but that was going to be short-lived as on my check round I found that the foresail sheet was a bit sick. I said to Jim that it would hang on for a couple of hours, as I didn't want to disturb Bob. I then decided to drop the foresail as the sheet area was very wet, and hung it in the breeze to dry.

Once the sheet was dry enough to work on, we made a brew and with the cuppa and following Bob's return to the deck it was decided to heave to, which would allow us to work with a bit of comfort. The mainsail was hove up a little more to keep the balance now that the foresail was down, and we shoved her round on the other tack leaving the jib made fast to windward.

The old girl lay as quiet as a duck and we had no spray or anything coming aboard. Bob was working very fast with his palm and needle, with Jim and me assisting when we could and learning a lot. Soon Bob announced that all was ready and I was then able to shackle the sheet back on with a good lashing of grease then it was up foresail, let draw the jib and once more the old girl was making headway.

After the repairs were completed we slacked away a bit more mainsail to balance the headsails, and then a little later Bob decided to give her all the main as the wind had fallen a bit further. Jim stood back aft and said to Bob, 'Look at the blue sky out there to windward, Skip.' 'Yes,' replied Bob 'Away lad and set the topsail,' so Jim got the job of nipping aloft and unstowing the topsail. Once Jim had returned to the deck we hadn't long to wait before the dark clouds had rolled away and the sky opened up to a lovely blue. The wind even went to the west-north-west so we could expect to make better progress and Bob left the deck to me and Jim.

As we closed the land the winds fell very light, but we were still making progress as we had the tide with us. When the tide turned and we started a backwards drift, I told Jim to drop the headsails and we then let go the anchor. We lay a couple of miles offshore with the anchor on the ground, our fishing lines over the side and myself with a book. We were able to let Bob have a good sleep.

Jim had got a nice bit of grub ready before we needed to call Bob, and I had four nice codling to my credit, so things were looking good. Just before the low water we hove the anchor up, and after setting up the bobstay we were able to double jib the old girl and slowly creep up along the land with just a gentle breeze playing with us. That was how, hour by hour, we headed south until we turned to the west and arrived off our berth at Harwich gas works. There was not enough wind to take us into our berth, so once again we were at the mercy of a fisherman. This time the tow was just ten shillings, a far cry from the ten pounds at Bridlington, but the conditions were somewhat different.

Once again the hold was empty and Jim and I had enjoyed a good run ashore and written all the letters to our different girls. This time we knew our orders. They were that we should go back north to Keadby and load coal for a Colchester discharge. I hadn't heard from Bob, but had left a message with his wife the day before to say that we would be ready for sea the next day. True to form, he jumped aboard just before high water.

Jim and I started dashing about getting the topsail and mainsail set. Bob asked how we were going to get out of the creek. I said that if we kept one mooring line aft she should swing and then when we slipped it we should be away. He said, 'Right, let's see if it works.' Bob was always trying you at little things like that, but I was very confident that it would work, so when we were nearly round I gave Jim the nod to slip the rope and the old girl went forward like a greyhound unleashed. Jim then nipped along and set the foresail.

Bob said, 'Perfect. Now go along and get her set up forward.' That meant getting the bowsprit down and the jib set. By the time we had the Guard buoy abeam it was harden everything in, and with the wind from the south-west, the *Greenhithe* was off on her best point of sailing, close-hauled. We had all her sails set. 'Maybe a little too much sail,' said Bob, 'but as we clear the Landguard Point we'll be bearing away so she will carry it more easily.'

We were sloshing away across the harbour and all seemed set fair when a ferry decided to make us wind before we needed. That gave Bob something to swear about. I had spotted a pilot cutter which seemed to be making a close run for our stern. Bob didn't worry about him, but still he kept coming. Then all of a sudden he eased down and spoke with us. He told us that we had a change of orders. We were to go to the London Tunnel cement works and load a cargo of cement for Colchester.

That really gave Bob good reason to swear as the tide was no good for us now, and we would have to bring up. As soon as we had anchored we got the fishing gear out. We were not very far from the Stonebanks buoy, a good fishing spot. Jim and I spent some time down in the hold as we had to be very clean for loading the cement. When we thought we were going to load coal, it hadn't been necessary to sweep out too carefully.

Just before low water Bob said, 'Right lads, get her underway and away you go.' That meant he was doing some scribbling, as he termed it, so Jim and I got the anchor up and setting the bobstay tight, we soon had the jib drawing nicely and the old *Greenhithe* was really going well. Bob put in an appearance after a couple of hours. He said that he could see that we were doing okay, so he would leave us to it and if we wanted him, to give him a shout. Jim and I didn't have to call Bob and we both knew he was probably writing, or asleep, and could be called at very short notice if needed.

We both knew that Bob's intention was to keep going as long as we could and lady luck was with us for a time. The wind had done nothing except back from the southward since we had got underway. I said to Jim that I reckoned the wind would freshen up, but I got that bit wrong. The wind got around to about the east-south-east and stayed about a force four or five, just in favour of the *Greenhithe*. We were going up the Swin at a rate of knots. Bob put in an appearance again at about high water as he expected we would have to bring up, but as we were going well I suggested that he should stay below out of our way and perhaps our luck would hold!

Our wind was to stay with us for quite a time. We were at the top of Sea Reach before the wind headed us so that we had to anchor. We knew then that, with luck, we should berth on the tide at the Tunnel Cement works. Jim and I stowed the bowsprit up and got a couple of hours' sleep. When next it was time for us to get at it, Bob was calling us with a nice cup of tea. We lit the navigation lights and then once again it was heave up and let's away.

Shortly after our arrival we learned that we had to go into the inside berth to load. That meant we couldn't get into there until half flood, and if we didn't get loaded before the high water we would be stuck until the next flood. It was not possible to get out of there on the ebb as the tide ran so hard and the jetty lay athwart the tide. Again our luck held, we managed to get our head down just before high water, and so once again we were bound outwards. The bowsprit was down with the jib set up on it and we knew that with a good five hours tide and wind about force five from the south-east, *Greenhithe* was certainly on her way. Bob managed to keep us going and it wasn't until we were in the River Colne near the mouth of Pyefleet Creek that at last we had to stow up. Down went the anchor and we all had a few hours turned in.

On turning out it was for Jim and me to stow up the bowsprit and gear and generally make ready for discharge. When it was time for us to heave up it was but a short sail from Pyefleet up to the mooring buoys just below James Cook's Wivenhoe shipyard. We were picked up by the little local motor boat and towed the final couple of miles up to Colchester Hythe. Bob was away as soon as we had moored up, for he hadn't been able to get home on our last trip to London. Colchester was a good place for him to get home from. Unloading gave us a couple of days at Colchester and Jim and I made good use of our time ashore.

Coal from the North, back to Colchester gas works, were our next orders. We had followed our discharge with the brooms and would be ready to load as soon as we got there. Our mail that had not by then been sent to Harwich had been redirected to Colchester, so Jim and I had a quick bit of writing to do to keep our ladies happy!

102 As the small motor boat came alongside we gave him a turn whilst we singled up. We hadn't seen Bob yet but we knew he would soon board, and with the sun shining and a light breeze from the south-west we were keen to be off. The barge had just about lifted off the bottom when Bob stepped aboard saying to Jim, 'What's the kettle doing, mate?'

Jim knew that meant tea was Bob's priority. And to me it was, 'Everything okay, mate?' and I said, 'Yes. We'd better let go then.'

As we towed down river Bob told me that the London area trade was very bad and we had to think ourselves lucky that we had the coal run to keep us going. I didn't mind it myself except that from Colchester to Keadby was about one hundred and eighty miles, and that's a long way to go empty in a cranky sailing barge. That was why we always hoped for reasonable weather.

By the time we had towed down to Alresford we had all the sails set and had even lowered the bowsprit. With a shout from the tug it was let go the towrope. Jim and I got the anchor hove on the bow, the bobstay tight, and set the two jibs up, but the wind was very fickle and the old girl just sort of ambled along without making too much progress. As it was just coming up to high water we hadn't any tide to help. After clearing the Colne the tide was nicely away with us. We had a steady breeze out of the south-west and once again we were beginning to settle into a seagoing routine and looking forward to a nice easy-going trip.

That was not to be, because when Jim had gone aft with a mug of tea for Bob he had quietly said to him that there was another sail ahead of us, just cleared Harwich, that had shaped away north. Bob went forward to take a look himself, came aft a bit quick and said we must get the big balloon jib up and set. He was certain that it could only be one barge, the *Will Everard*, and he would bet that she was bound for Keadby.

Bob knew that we had very little chance of catching the 'Will', but I think he just wanted the challenge of the race. Jim and I joined in the spirit of the contest. At dark the 'Will' was still only about a mile ahead of us and we seemed to be holding him.

No lights did we see from the 'Will' all night so we couldn't really see what he was up too. Nobody got much sleep for we all wanted to get the best from the old girl, and that meant trimming the sails at frequent intervals. Towards dawn I went along to the bow to see if I could see anything of the 'Will', but no. So then I nipped up aloft and when I was about thirty feet off the deck I could just make

The *Will Everard* was the adversary for the 'race' down to Keadby, and the wager on the way back.

out her sails. Bob reckoned he was a good couple of miles ahead. It was then that we began to doubt if we could catch him, but we still had a long way to go. Bob said we must not give up until the first of us arrived at Keadby.

By the time we got to the Humber the 'Will' was still a couple of miles ahead of us. We brought up that night as the tide finished, to the west of Read's Island, five miles above Barton. Bob said that the 'Will' would have made it to Keadby.

Early on the next day's tide we arrived alongside the 'Will' at Keadby before any loading started, so although we were beaten it was no disgrace. Both the 'Will' and Greenhithe were soon loaded. The 'Will' was lying on the outside of us, having loaded first. When the big tug the Waterman arrived to tow us down it was the 'Will' that went on the towing hook first, and us on the stern of her. John, the mate of the 'Will', and I had decided that we would have a race back to Colchester and the loser would buy the beer for the other crew for the one evening. That was going to cost one of us quite a bit of money.

I had made Bob aware of the wager whilst we were towing down but he just laughed, 'Right, mate, we'll give it our best shot.' I knew that Bob loved the challenge of a race. Once free of the tug and below Hull we were close by the 'Will' just off Killingholme when Bob took the chance to push through her lee. Laughing he said, 'I don't think that it will be for long,' but Bob had the bit between his teeth and for the rest of the run out of the Humber we managed to stay ahead of them.

Going across the Wash the 'Will' was going well to the inside of us. Bob decided we would keep off up the inside of the Race Bank to get a better run of tide. As we closed Cromer the 'Will' was only about a mile ahead; the old Greenhithe was trying her best.

As the daylight turned to darkness I was called from a watch below. Bob turned her over to me as the ebb had started to run. I had to watch her all the time and, as the wind was tending to be more westerly, we had the chance to make a little more on the 'Will' as I crept along close to the shore on the lead line. The 'Will' was well off from us and so had more tide to push. Bob had a good sleep for all was quiet and clear and, as the race was my challenge, I was glad to be the one in control through that lovely night.

Dawn seemed to come around very quickly and Bob put his nose out of the hatch saying, 'Kettle's on, mate!' and soon he came up with a couple of mugs of steaming hot and very sweet tea. He said, 'I think we'll have the boy out now, for this race is going to keep us busy today.' After a very good breakfast I was told to go get a couple of hours' rest. I said to Bob that as we had such a good start to the day, and knowing that the area we were entering was Bob's home waters, I wanted to see the best way of handling it.

As we approached Lowestoft, Bob was up to his tricks for he called for the lead and we went right in with just a couple of inches under the leeboard. The water was very smooth and since Bob had taken the watch his last little bit of juggling had once again put us ahead of the 'Will'.

Out of nowhere we suddenly had a very heavy squall and our topmast had a bad case of the nods. I nipped out of the wheelhouse and put a handy billy preventer on the running backstay, but both of us knew we were over canvassed with the two jibs on the bowsprit. Bob didn't say reduce anything and for about another five minutes all was well and were charging. Suddenly another squall hit us, and the starboard crosstree buckled forward.

Without any shout at all from Bob, I was on the mast deck and had dropped the staysail down. I told the third hand to stand by the topsail halyards but to release them only should Bob give the shout. I dived down the fo'c'sle as an idea had flashed through my mind as I grabbed our cargo wire. Regaining the deck I cut through the lashings and took the end which had the eye in it aloft with me. I also slipped a shackle into the eye.

On gaining the masthead I had to clamber out along the crosstree. Reaching the end, I sat on it long enough to pass the eye of the wire around it and shackle it on to its own part. Then, sliding down to the deck via the standing backstay, I was along aft like some machine. Taking a couple of turns around the barrel of the crab-winch[1] Jim and I had soon bent the crosstree back to where it should have been, I looked at Bob and he said, 'Right, let's have the staysail over the jib,' and that was quickly set aloft once more.

Going aft once more, our Jim said, 'I think we'll have a cup of tea to celebrate.' As he gained the deck, Bob went below and brought the whisky bottle up to lace the tea, and asked what made me think of that. All I could answer was, 'I don't know Bob, but I didn't want us looking at the 'Will's stern.'

Bob commented that if the wind didn't free any further we didn't have much hope the other side of Orfordness. Of course, the wind showed no sign of freeing and so the 'Will' was once again to draw past us. As the tide finished in our favour the 'Will' brought up on the Naze and we were in Dovercourt Bay.
As the evening flood started to trickle in we slowly got our anchor hove up and set the lot again for the last part of our race. A race that we knew we had lost unless the Will got stranded or something. We went tack for tack up the Wallet with the bigger craft. As we passed by the Inner Bench Head buoy the 'Will' was putting up his riding light and so that put us second best after a race of some one hundred and eighty miles. Bob's comment was that you'll never get a closer contest than that. We were unlikely to have the chance to race the Will Everard again as she was soon to go on the shipyard at Greenhithe to have an auxiliary engine installed.

Jim and I had known that we would be at Colchester for about four days that trip, so we had got Bob to bring up just clear of the Inner Bench Head. Out went the fishing gear and we fished for about three hours. By the time we turned in we had caught enough fish for Bob to be able to take a feed home for the family.

Next day saw us on the back of the motor boat again but with the 'Will' in between us. We both swung, ready for the off from the old gas works, with

[1] One of a pair of winches fixed either side of the barge aft, used to raise and lower the leeboards, and fitted with a multi-function barrel for other purposes.

the *'Will'* being the first in the discharge berth. That evening we went ashore just after seven, so it looked as if it was going to cost me a few bob. However, by nine o'clock the crew of the *'Will'* decided that they'd had enough free beer and bought me a couple, but the bet had been honoured.

As Bob stepped aboard for our run we already knew that we had to go North again empty for more coal. Jim and I didn't have to sweep the hold out and everything else was ready as Bob came back. He was well early as he had

news for our Jim. The 'powers that be' wanted Jim for the mate's berth in the *Lady Maud*, but they had reckoned without our Jim. In no way would he hear of it. I still think that the prospect of pump or sink dispelled any thoughts Jim might have had of going mate on anything made of wood.

Bob popped ashore to make the phone call to the office to let them know Jim's answer. He also checked our orders, but they were still the same. The motor boat was on time as usual and he gave us a good run down well clear of Alresford. Once

Third Hand Jim decided to turn down an offer of promotion to mate aboard the wooden *Lady Maud*, seen here on the London River.

we had let him go we picked up a nice breeze from the west and this was to stay with us for the whole trip north. It was a perfect passage with the watches going four on and four off. I do believe it was the only trip that ever went like that. We had to pick up a tug in Hull Roads as we ended the trip with no wind at all.

Loading at Keadby was always a pleasure and the beer in the Friendship was very good. As it was still calm when we had loaded, Bob decided that we would have a night where we were and would see what the next day might bring.

In the morning the Humber tug arrived in good time and had started us away before high water. By the time we were in Hull Roads we had nearly a full ebb before us. As we got the bowsprit on her Bob said not to set the staysail up as we were going to have plenty of wind before the day was out, and he was right. Still, it did us some good, for when the wind did come it was out of the north. The old girl had to have the topsail down, but even so was making very good time. What we didn't like was that as the day went on, the wind was slowly backing. By the time we were off Cromer we also got the jib off her and were down to just foresail and a few cloths less than the full main. The *Greenhithe* was in then her 'safe rig' and we were hove to with the wind from the south-west and blowing a moderate gale. We spent a lot of the night looking out of the companion hatches, when we hadn't got our heads down.

Daylight found us still with the same weather, but Bob let us draw as the tide made to the south, and by the next high water we were at least getting some lee from the Scroby Sands. We had quite a comfortable day, touching the anchor down after a couple of hours to await the fair tide, while we all fell to for a nice bit of grub and a few hours sleep.

As the tide went so did the wind fall, but by the time we were underway for our next tide we had west-north-west, about a force five and gusting. The prospects looked a lot better for us and although we were still under a reduced rig we were making very good progress. Later, flying up past the Orfordness lighthouse with the lot set, Bob said that we would have to bring up before we got to Harwich. The tide was going to be running hard out and the wind was still not free enough to allow us to sail into the harbour against the ebb.

Still, we got as far as just clear of Wadgate Ledge buoy above Felixstowe pier, when it was again time to stow up and drop the anchor. We lay in a nice quiet anchorage and were all able to turn in for a full watch below.

On the low water we were underway again with a nice fetch up to Harwich on the starboard tack. A few boards saw us rounding the Guard buoy, and then away on the starboard tack until we were up abreast of the gasworks creek. We had shortened sail as we reached up the river and Bob bore away and shaped to run into the creek. We knew that at this state of the tide we would hit the mud before we had water into our berth. A couple of fishing boats were in our berth. We dropped the topsail, and when Bob's shout came Jim and I dropped a leeboard each to bring us to a halt just short of the wharf. As the tide made in, the fishing boats left and we just put our mooring ropes ashore and tended the old girl into the berth, before we made ready for discharge.

Next morning the crane was slamming into us at about six o'clock so we had an early morning cuppa. On asking why the early start, the wharf men told us that they had a ship due on the next tide and they wanted to get us out of the way before it arrived. They discharged our cargo very quickly, so we had just to swing clear and then think about how to get out, as the wind was blowing straight into the creek.

The 'ship' turned out to be our firm's little wooden motor vessel, the *Assurity*, which had arrived carrying no more than ourselves. He came in stern first, took a rope off us and gave us a very good pull over to the Shotley shore. From there we were able to get the mainsail and topsail set whilst he held us into the wind. On letting the tow rope go Bob was able to bear away and shape for the Guard buoy.

Slackening all the sheets off, we were soon flying along out of the harbour bound for Colchester. The indications were that we should have a fair wind up to the Inner Bench Head buoy at the mouth of the River Colne. Bob therefore didn't have the bowsprit down as we had plenty of time to push the ebb along the shore.

Jim and I spent a lot of time getting the hold swept clean, although Bob didn't know what we were loading. He reckoned it would be grit, but he wasn't very convincing, telling me that we would only find out when we got up there.

We brought up just outside the Colne. Jim and I would have liked to have done a bit of fishing but we hadn't a scrap of bait. So, although we were lying in a good spot, we could only think about it. As we began to swing athwart on the low water it was once again time to heave short and get under way. A few tacks got us up to the mooring buoys at Fingringhoe, there to moor and lie for the remainder of the night. In those days the River Colne was not worked in the dark.

Next day Bob's mystery was revealed. We were going to load a cargo of straw for Ridham Dock off the Swale behind the Isle of Sheppey in Kent. I'm sure Bob knew before we had left Harwich and just kept it as a surprise. Once we were told, he outlined the work involved in loading the cargo and how to make it show us a profit. One of our firm's barges was loading straw when we

A gentle breeze carries the *Greenhithe* to her berth.

arrived, so I was able to go aboard and see how sail sheeting arrangements had to be altered to allow things to work with a 'stack' towering above our deck. Also I was able to see the method of lashing the cargo down.

I spent quite some time giving the other barge crew a hand to create their 'stack'. It was a bit like loading timber, in that after the hold is full it is battened down. But then things become different, as a heavy wire with a piece of timber below it was rigged up and over the fore and main horses. The wire was hove tightly by the use of a bottle screw. A few rough reefs are needed in the mainsail and foresail but remarkably they still give the boat a reasonable performance.

When our turn came to load I had gained quite a grasp of the methods. The *Greenhithe*, having a large hold, was able to swallow a good tonnage below her decks. Before he left for home Bob told me not to cover the hold. The result of that guidance was that our stack was much easier to build. The big slope of our hatches would otherwise have made things very difficult. The lads on the quay at Colchester also gave us plenty of good advice. We ended up with something like thirty-nine tons of straw according to our loading documents, and looked like a floating haystack when we were ready for sea.

A phone call from me alerted Bob who arrived to sail on the tide. As Bob stepped on board he had a very good laugh at our ship. I didn't really know if he wanted just to tie us up in some creek somewhere, and let a few cows get rid of the stack.

The motor boat pulling us away brought another laugh. One of us had to stand on the top of the stack to 'take the con'. We were going down the river like an out of control plough and carving a little from each bank as we went. Once we had let go of the tug we had to get down to the serious job of trying to sail. It seemed a lot easier once we were on compass courses. Our wind going out to the Spitway was a fine east north-east so that with the ebb beneath us we were making very good and steady progress.

Once we had passed through the Spitway we had a good running wind. Although it was wind over tide, with the freeboard that we had with such a light cargo we were very unlikely to put any water on our decks. By the time we had got up around the Blacktail Spit, the tide was easing, and the old girl was once again going well. We were then going across the swell and with our large stack the barge had a very heavy and slow roll; enough to make you wonder what she would have been like if it had been rough. It wasn't far to Sheerness and that's where we were shaping up for.

Entering Sheerness we had to be very vigilant, for there were plenty of obstructions that we had to avoid – mooring buoys and anchored craft – and also plenty of craft moving around. Fortunately, most vessels underway gave way to us, mainly I suspect, to give themselves a good laugh at our antics, but at a safe distance.

110   When our haystack was ashore Bob told us we were going to load cement from Bevens Wharf at Greenhithe for an unknown destination. We had a hell of a job in the breeze trying to sweep out the hold and clearing it of all the straw, which kept on wanting to go its own way. As fast as we got it into heaps away it went again, but at last we beat it.

By the time we got to Bevens there was no trace of straw left. The wharf foreman said that they would load us during the night. The ten o'clock shift started us and finished sometime in the early hours, whilst we were still turned in. We turned out very early and prepared the *Greenhithe* for sea. Bob had said that he would go to our yard in the morning and pick up a few things that we needed, and he came back aboard by the motor boat with news that we were bound for Colchester.

As we were ready to depart we passed a rope to the motor boat which was able to pull us well clear of the bight, as by then the tide was running very fast. When setting our canvas after loading cement you could always feel the cement dust grinding through the blocks, so the old oil can and the grease was out and I had to spend quite a lot of time aloft to clear things up there too.

The wind was from the east north-east so we could not expect an easy run. I knew that with Bob on board we would not lie anywhere for long, he would have much preferred to have lain at Greenhithe and gone home. After we had messed about quite a bit and were going through the lower part of Gravesend Reach, Bob said that he wished that he had stayed at home. The wind had freshened a lot and he said we would have to bring up on the flood and were unlikely to be going down any further on the next ebb. I thought to myself that he was telling me this because he was going to anchor at Gravesend and go back home. But no, he kept us going, and finally we got to between the Chapman Head light and Southend pier. There we were to lie all the next day as well, for there wasn't any sign of a let up in the weather.

We put the day to good use fishing, and those fish were grabbing our baits like there was no tomorrow, which in reality there wasn't for them. Early the next day Bob called us saying we were going to have a go. The wind was no finer and there had been no change in its direction. However, Bob kidded himself that it was a little better so we whipped the old anchor up as things came slack and we were off on a long beat down. We had one jib on the bowsprit, the head of the topsail down, and with the main brails hove tight, we were making reasonable progress. As the wind freshened we had to reduce the mainsail and drop the jib.

We were just above the South West Middle buoy as low water approached and we were to spend the next flood tide there, where the old girl lay very well. Just before the high water we were ready to get underway. The squalls were very heavy as they went through whilst we got sorted out. Bob just gave her our usual 'storm rig' and we slowly but surely made our way down towards the Spitway. As we went through, Bob said we could be short of water, but he managed to keep the old girl going. As we got a good lee from the Gunfleet Sand we passed through the Spitway smoothly. When we got into deep water the other side it was a different story. There was a very heavy swell running. The cement in our holds made the old *Greenhithe* let us know that she could roll, and running towards the Knoll buoy the water was tumbling aboard and rushing the length of our decks. By the time we hauled into the River Colne we were washed as clean as a new pin.

As the wind was fair, Bob decided that we would go on up to the moorings at Fingringhoe. We pushed along over the ebb tide and just below Fingringhoe, about halfway through Marriages Bight, Bob got it wrong and we touched to leeward. She wouldn't come off so all we could do was to stow up and get below in the warm. Nothing could harm us there, so instead of having to moor up we just put up the anchor light and turned in for a while.

On the next tide the motor boat came to us quite early and slipped us off the edge of the bank and began the short haul to Colchester. Bob caught his train home and Jim and I made ready for discharge. The weather was not very good for the first couple of days for it didn't stop raining. We spent most of the time in the Anchor pub on the quay and got wet inside as well as out!

I had wandered along the quay to the brokers' office, Francis and Gilders. I was having a quiet chat with the clerk when Mr Josh Francis came into the room and asked me through to the inner office. Having got me seated he then told me all about how he was Skipper of a barge when he was seventeen; then came his bomb-shell. He offered me a Skipper's berth. I was really taken aback and I said I'd have to think about it. When I said about the difference of him starting at the age of twelve and me starting at the age of

Mr Josh Francis of the Colchester barge owners Francis & Gilders. who offered Ivan a Master's job in one of his craft.

thirteen and ten months, he pointed out that where I had been coasting all the time, his work had been mostly confined to the river.

I went into the outer office where they had a phone booth from where crews from visiting craft could make a call, the charges being picked up on our final bill. Bob was in when I got through, and his few seconds silence when I told him what I had been offered seemed to last an age. He said that I should take it with open arms and, even if I only did one trip to get my Master's C.C. (Customs Certificate) discharge, it would stand well to my credit, and he assured me that I could do it. I laughingly said that he only wanted to get rid of me, and he said, 'You can always come back if you don't like it.'

And so, full of apprehension, I accepted Mr Francis' offer. When the last of our cargo was out I was paid off, and over a couple of pints Bob gave me a last few valuable bits of advice.

Chapter XIII
MY FIRST COMMAND

As with any major decision that comes along in life, one is bound to be apprehensive, but for a lad who was only just eighteen years old such concerns were overidden by the excitement of the moment. I was about to take command of a sailing barge and I was over the moon.

I had offered Jim the mate's berth but he declined. He also declined Bob's offer to take the mate's berth in the *Greenhithe*, so Bob shipped a lad from Greenhithe way.

As there were a couple of days before I was to take over my first command, I was able to have some time at home, there to replenish the washing and see some of the lads.

The small yard of Francis and Gilders lay just above the Hythe Road Bridge, and what a shock I received when I arrived there on that bleak Monday morning of 20th November 1947. The hull that lay in the mud was bare. Just ashore were the spars and rigging. Further up the field the sails were thrown in a heap. I was tempted to walk off the yard and go and seek another berth, but

The new Master having just shipped aboard his first command at Colchester.

after some thought I decided to look upon it as a challenge. With the backing of the yard master, who was one of the firm's directors, I knew we could round her up. The cabin hadn't had anyone using it for some time, so I kept a very good fire aboard for a week to allow the place to dry and air out thoroughly, and went home to Ipswich each night.

Next on my list was to find myself a reasonable mate, but the craft was small, carrying only one hundred and twenty tons to sea, so to sail by the share I wasn't going to find it easy. Any rate, I found a lad who I'd known since school days and duly signed him on in the logbook as mate, beneath my own name with the rank of Master. His rate of pay was stated as two pounds and ten shillings (£2.50) a week for time on the yard, and my own was to be four pounds. This rate was as good as any at the time so I thought that things were set fair. Unfortunately my mate had different ideas, as after he had been with me for just three days he asked me if I would sub him three pounds to allow him to get some oilskins and boots. Like a fool I said yes and passed over the three pounds. At least I made him sign for the money just in case anything went wrong. Next day he was nowhere to be seen.

After plenty of asking around the usual haunts, it seemed that he had disappeared off the face of the earth! It was to be quite a few years before I was able to catch up with him. Then I was in a position to twist his arm and got a fiver back shortly after he paid off his ship.

His replacement was better than I could ever have hoped to find, for it was my old friend 'Tintack'. He had done as much barging as I had but he didn't want any responsibility. He was a first-class seaman, although prone to seasickness when the going got really rough.

We got stuck into the work and the old lady soon began to look like a barge again. We had cleaned up the spars and then shipped them aboard. We soon had them aloft instead of lying in the field. After dressing the sails and tarring the bolt ropes around the edge of the sails, it was just a question of getting them all dried out before we could ship them aboard and bend them on. Meanwhile, 'Tintack' and I worked hard at cleaning her down over the side, and made some attempt to tar the sides, but there was a lot of mud in the berth which didn't help.

At last came the great day, and after making sure we had got paraffin oil and various other stores on board, we had to lower the gear down, before poking through the Hythe Bridge and getting moored up just below.

After mooring at the quay we had to rig our little ship again, and that time we knew that when the gear was up we would be ready for our first cargo. Just as when I was in the *George Smeed*, we stood for the priority turn coming off the yard. But I don't think it would have made a great deal of difference on that occasion as we were the only Francis and Gilders craft at Colchester. We had orders to load one hundred and twenty tons of grit for Bow Creek, which was going to be a nice little start for us.

Anyone who has worked up to the old East Mills at Colchester will know that it is really hard graft, and 'Tintack' and I decided we should avoid it if possible. I knew that we were the class of barge for that run, so I could expect to be called upon to load for there occasionally. If the tides were neaps there wouldn't be enough water for a barge to get up to the Mill, so then we would have to lie at Colchester Quay on demurrage. A lot of the older Skippers used to like that.

The *Saltcote Belle*, for that was the name of my first command, was a very stable craft with very flat sides and in a blow would stand up like a church and put the weight into her spars. I was used to the *'Smeed'* and the *Greenhithe* which in the same conditions would just lie down, and the wind would go over the top of them. This difference in character took a lot of getting used to.

When we were coming to the end of our loading it gave me great pleasure to be able to go along to the office and order my tug away, to collect a sub, and to sign for it beneath where it said Master. The tug arrived alongside and I signed the slip to say he could be paid, and so it was about an hour before high water that we at last got away. To 'Tintack' it was just another trip, but to me it was the all-important first trip in command.

Casting away from the tug just below Marriages Bight, I began to get the feel of the *Saltcote Belle* and how different she turned out to be. Even tacking through the wind she kept going, and that's where she beat me. We had got well down below Freshwater Jetty when I shouted lee ho, and before she came around the leeboard had shot up and much to my disgust the bugger would not come off. All we could do was to stow up, and I was as low and disgusted as I could be with myself, more than ever before. But 'Tintack' had the right idea saying, 'Let's turn in, mate; can't float till there's water,' and I'll always think of that day and thank him for those few words that put things into perspective for me.

A couple of hours before the high water we were well afloat and were off with a nice fair wind. It was a fine staysail breeze and we were making good progress. True to form with our settled summer highs, we could nearly always expect wind off the land in the morning, wind on the land in the afternoon. We were over and through the Spitway before the wind shifted into the south-east so we still had a fair wind but on the other tack.

Making up nicely along the Shoebury shore we were to finally lose the wind altogether at the West Shoebury buoy, so that's where we had to put the pick in the ground and to lie until we got a breeze. The night tide brought us no wind at all, so I said to 'Tintack', 'I'm not messing about drudging[1] all night so we'll turn in and lie the night, and see what the morning brings for us.'

Turning out next morning we found a nice light breeze out of the north, so we had a quick brew up, then hove up the anchor and got the old girl going again. Whilst sailing along up Sea Reach we were able to give ourselves a good

[1] Drudging is a means of moving the barge in a fair tide and no wind. The anchor is kept just touched on the ground so that the barge is carried astern with, but slower than, the tide. The rudder remains effective and can sheer the barge, to dictate her course.

Ivan at the wheel, with the mate for'ard quanting over the side, drifting through Colchester.

hearty breakfast. As the day went on so the wind freshened, and as it was in our favour we were quite happy. On the last of the flood we were only at the top of Long Reach but we kept going until we were able to draw into the bight at Erith. Then it was down anchor again to await the next slack tide on the low water.

Before the slack, 'Tintack' had turned out and made the tea, so we could have a nice easy cuppa and a fag before heaving up. Getting underway was quick, for the *Saltcote Belle* was quite an easy craft for us two young fellows to handle. It wasn't very long before we had run up onto the lighter roads just outside Bow Creek and my first run as Master was satisfactorily completed. In the morning we were able to get a tosher to give us a pluck up into our berth in the creek.

It was a thrill for me to see my first cargo going out, and to know that I had coped with my responsibilities as Master. I was beginning to think I could meet the challenge. It was the usual thing for the Master to slip up to our city office whilst in the London area if time permitted and, as it did on that occasion, I thought I'd go and see the man who did all the seeking on our behalf. He turned out to be a very decent chap and was able to give me a lot of advice about how the system worked, and said he would load us for anywhere as I requested. I was most impressed with Mr Vandersite, but he hadn't any orders for us.

By the time I arrived back at the wharf the gent in the ticket office came out and said our London office had asked me to call. I then spoke with Mr Vandersite again, who told me he had orders for us to go to the Surrey Commercial Dock to load timber for Heybridge Basin. I clambered aboard to let 'Tintack' know the good news.

Getting out of the creek was no problem. I just held a line up as a tosher came near. They would find out which way you wanted to go, and then the dollar or quarter of tea would be all that was needed.

We found ourselves out in the river with no wind at all. We drudged up through Blackwall Reach and, as we entered Greenwich Reach, one of the police boats going up put his stern just inside our sternpost and gave us a shove to the dock pier head. Having got a turn, I asked the police if there was anything they needed. They asked if we had any tinned milk to spare; it seemed we could always find something when needed. We were often subject to a search in the docks, but nobody that I knew was ever fined for having gear that they shouldn't have had on board.

We took a turn on one of a group of lighters and then, as they were towed into the lock, we were hove in with them. Going out the other end into the dock we were all just towed through the inner gate and left to our own devices to get clear. That meant running the dolly wire away and heaving like mad to try and find a way through the lighters to get to the ship that you were going to load from.

All the London docks were full of ships in those days and likewise full of lighters with nobody to worry over them. The lightermen were in the café or in the pub, and nearly half the delays to a ship were caused by the lightermen not being there to look after their craft. The other half were caused by the dockers stopping to strike, wanting more money for dirt, or any excuse they could find. We had to wait a week to load the cargo and that meant we would be on demurrage before we left the dock. Being an 'import' cargo, we only had to allow them four days to load and discharge.

A nip up the city was called for to get a sub and have a chat with our broker. There was really nothing at Heybridge Basin where we were bound. There was a pub, of course, and to obtain a sub normally meant phoning the office and asking them to send the money to the pub. The landlord there did sub some of the Skippers himself, but this was risky for him and I think he lost out on quite a few occasions.

'Tintack' and myself spent quite a few nights in the Prince of Orange just outside the dock gates whilst we were loading. The pub was very lively, the beer good, and there was no need to walk very far to get back when we were 'half cut'.

Loading a barge in the London docks had to be done by the London dockers, who were well paid to do it. But in the case of barges I think the barge crew did about sixty per cent of the loading and the dockers the rest. If we didn't use our knowledge of proper stowage methods we would never have loaded the full amount of cargo. We often had a lot of work to do after the dockers had gone home, which 'Tintack' and I took in our stride. After the loading was completed, it was up to us to get all the wire lashings sorted and all the tackles set up to enable us to keep our stack in tight.

The mainsail and foresail were altered to clear the stack. In our type of barge we took the main brails off the winch and used the dolly winch to heave the mainsail up. That allowed us to run lengths of timber right through the mastdeck and gain more tonnage. *Saltcote Belle* was a good barge for timber work, her hold being full and square. We were then ready for sea. We had only three tides to get out before incurring extra dock charges, so we hove ourselves down the dock and waited on the pier heads for a lock out.

Next morning, after the locking in was done, we were amongst the first into the lock ready to go out. Setting our sails as the outer gates opened, we sailed straight out into the river. Getting away like that, and with a fair wind, we were able to be at the top end of Woolwich Reach before the tide turned in our favour. But sailing down, with the wind being very fickle all day, we could only make the low water just below the West Blyth buoy so we brought up there to await the next tide.

We turned to for a bit of grub below and then a couple of hours' rest on the locker. The high water came and it was time to make sail again with just a nice steady breeze from the south-west. When we had the anchor short and shipped our lights, we set all sail. Breaking the anchor away, I left 'Tintack' to get it on the bow, and walked aft to take the wheel and to imagine I was on my own big yacht.

'Tintack' made our next brew, and then I told him to go and have a couple more hours on the locker. When he left the deck we had the wind about force three and the visibility was great. I told myself that this was about the best life could be, sailing along like aboard a pleasure yacht, and getting paid for it.

Going down past the West Middle buoy, I called 'Tintack' out again. He made more tea, coming on deck with two steaming mugs before he took over the watch. He asked about the depth of water in the Spitway and I assured him he would have plenty. With our timber cargo we were only drawing four feet six inches aft and there should be at least nine feet through there at low water.

Later on 'Tintack' gave me a call, so I put the kettle on and made the next brew. On gaining the deck I found that we had lost all our wind, but were through the Spitway and up to the Knoll buoy. We had no option but to stow up and let go the anchor. I thought that if we got underway on the flood tide, without any wind, we would be driven up into the River Colne, so we stayed put and our next watch turned out to be eleven hours below.

At last the old bob[1] started to move. 'Tintack' and I set to and trimmed the sails and soon the old *'Belle'* was underway and reaching towards Osea Island up the Blackwater. At least we were going up the right river.

My mind turned to the procedures to be followed once we got up to Heybridge Basin. It proved to be fairly simple. Once we arrived off the Basin the ebb had just begun. I stowed up everything except the topsail and staysail. Then, drawing into the gut way to the lock approach, we dropped the topsail. By easing or pulling in the staysail sheet we were able to control our speed, Finally I shouted to 'Tintack', 'Down staysail.' and I let run the leeboards bringing us to a full stop. We put a couple of ropes out to stay ready for the next locking in.

We were very close to the Old Ship, which seemed a good place to spend our spare time whilst we waited for the next high water. We were to enjoy good beer there for the next few days.

When it was time for us to lock in, there was still a little breeze blowing straight into the lock. As the outer gate was pulled back ready for us, we just had to slack our ropes to blow ahead into the lock and then, as soon as they had the inner gate open, we just blew in to our berth just inside the knuckle of the lock. We got our headrope ashore and set the mizzen to blow our stern round and so lie head outward, ready for leaving once our cargo was ashore.

With a timber cargo to unload, a few planks at a time, there was very little for us to do whilst discharging, except boozing and catching up on plenty of lost sleep. Heybridge in those days was only a little sleepy hollow, and it took

[1] 'Bob' was the sailorman's name for the barge's house, or owner's, flag which was flown at the topmast truck.

Ivan finds time to have a smoke when aboard the *Saltcote Belle* in Heybridge Basin.

about four days to discharge our cargo before we were ready for the off again. Our next cargo was already lined up for us. We had to go to Colchester to load straw, and I wasn't really very pleased.

We left Heybridge on the high water and although we had a fair wind I knew we wouldn't save our tide up to Colchester. We had a fair wind from the south-west so had a good run out of the Blackwater and into the Colne, reaching the moorings just below Wivenhoe. Next day the little motor boat came to us early and we were soon returned to our home port.

Having done a cargo of straw whilst mate of the *Greenhithe* I should have known all about it but, alas, there were many pitfalls I hadn't anticipated. Firstly, there was our passenger. She had arrived on board after 'Tintack' and I had been home for the weekend. 'Tintack' had come back on the Sunday evening, and when I arrived back on board early on the Monday morning there he was sporting a very black eye and his newly acquired love. She wanted a trip back to her home port of Grays. It was not unusual at that time, for there were quite a few 'ladies' on the circuit. I didn't mind too much to start with.

Having loaded *Saltcote Belle* with her stack well above the deck, we did all the lashing down and clearing up that was needed before we could go to sea. Our newly acquired third hand didn't want to do much to earn her keep; she had started off on the wrong foot if she wanted me to be a friend to her.

The little motor boat gave us a very good start and we were nearly down to Freshwater Jetty before he gave us a hoot, the signal to let go. We had a smart breeze from the north-north-east, and the old barge was off like a good'un.

That was when my troubles were to start. With the stack in the way it was impossible to see ahead from the wheel. I was on top of the stack to give instructions to 'Tintack' at the helm, who should have been concentrating on maintaining the courses I gave him. He was in fact concentrating elsewhere, and we were going all over the place. All I was doing was shouting at him, something that I'd never had to do before.

As there was a fair bit of swell running we were doing a lot of yawing about. After we had passed through the 'low way', a ditch running south from the Knoll buoy which was used as a short cut, we would be looking to head for near the Whitaker Beacon.

I thought we would be okay then but that was not to be. I had gone up on the stack again to have a look for the South-West Middle buoy and had my hand on the weather vang for support. Suddenly, 'Tintack' gave us an accidental gybe and the weather vang became the lee one, leaving me half dangling over the side, which was a very unpleasant experience, to say the least.

I scrambled down to the deck and found that a bight of the mainsheet had hooked itself around the binnacle as we gybed and sent it crashing down to leeward. The glass of the compass was smashed, rendering it useless. It turned out that we were to do three trips without a proper compass before the insurance was settled and we had a repair done. Until then we had to use the little compass from the barge boat.

I had a bloody good go at 'Tintack' but it seemed to do little good. I told him and his floozie that when we got to Ridham Dock they could both go ashore, and I only wanted to see one of them come back aboard. Hopefully 'Tintack' would see sense.

Through Sheerness I told 'Tintack' that I would have to get up on the stack again and I wanted his proper co-operation and concentration. He promised he would give it. Moments later I was shouting to 'Tintack' to bear hard away, but nothing happened and there they were at it again, as the barge went hell for leather, straight towards an Admiralty buoy.

I leapt from the top of the stack, landed on the deck alongside 'Tintack', grabbed and spun the wheel. One of the spokes caught him just under the kneecap, so he was sent hopping for a few minutes, but we just cleared the buoy. He did wake up to his responsibilities from that moment, and stayed that way until we got up to Ridham Bridge.

It was very dark when we arrived there and the thing to do was to ease ourselves into a nice quiet anchorage for the rest of the night. After going below for some nosh and tea, I told the floozie she would be going home next day after we had docked. Then, of course, the old floodgates opened and the tears fell, and a right old row erupted between 'Tintack' and myself. Needless to say 'they' won, and I agreed as before to take her on to Grays, from where she came.

Sailing through the bridge early in the morning gave us an early arrival in Ridham Dock, and four hours later we could have been away empty, with the hold swept out. However, as our orders were to go to London light, with nothing in the offing, I decided to stay the night and to give Sittingbourne a look over. At Ridham, from down on the dockside, a little narrow gauge train used to run about once an hour to Sittingbourne and back, saving a good couple of miles walking each way.

Next day we got ourselves away at a good state of the tide. After we had cleared the Swale and slipped out of Sheerness we had a very comfortable sail up river to Grays. This was marred only by our passenger who had threatened to jump overboard as we had passed through Gravesend Reach. 'Tintack' grabbed

The *Saltcote Belle* in a nice staysail breeze, when a yacht barge in her later years.

her and more or less threw her down the cabin hatch. Apparently it was all to do with her not wanting to leave the barge. He even had to pull the cabin hatch over to keep her down there.

After anchoring and tidying up, when we were ready to go ashore we let her up. Whilst we were getting ready to get into our boat another crew was going off. As they passed they offered her a berth which she jumped at. She couldn't have had a very happy home life, as she didn't even want to nip home before going away again. Still that suited her, and when our paths crossed again about a month later she was still with the same craft and seemed to be enjoying life. I think that in later life she married not a bargeman, but one of the lads from the Royal Navy.

Chapter XIV
LOWER THE STICKS

Saltcote Belle was a barge that had been built with the idea of stack work in her heyday, but this was rather unusual by the time I was in her. Straw cargoes were not to my liking, although they paid good freightage rates relative to other cargoes. Our next cargo, however, was to be completely different.

After 'Tintack' and I had enjoyed a couple of pints it was time for us to give the office a ring. We received orders to go to the Victoria Dock to load wheat for Colchester, East Mills. This was a trip that we hadn't done before so we didn't know what to expect. Getting to the dock from Grays was easy, for we had a fair wind up the river. Once we had got in and passed through the Albert Dock Basin we had a breeze which we used to sail up through the Albert Dock and into the Victoria Dock.

We found our ship, but had to wait three days for our cargo. 'Tintack' and I were having a mutter about the time we spent working without pay, all the time spent without orders, and all the days spent sailing empty. We agreed that we had nearly had enough of it, but carried on nevertheless. Our time spent lying about had seemed to have been getting longer, hitting us in our pockets, so we had good cause to moan.

Still, we now had orders and I could nip up to the city and draw a sub. With the cash we could while away the time drifting between the Canning Town pubs, the Liverpool Arms or the Bridge House, both a couple of lively joints with plenty of song and dance acts to keep us amused.

Eventually we had our cargo, and we were off chasing down the docks to get away. The three tides import rule applied, and we also had to try and get to Colchester to catch the spring tides or we could find ourselves lying nearly two weeks waiting for enough water to get up to East Mills. Some of the old bargemen who lived thereabouts used to try and work it that way, so that they lay on Colchester Hythe on demurrage. It may have suited them, but I think 'Tintack' and I would have gone crazy with that kind of lie.

Once we had cleared the dock locks bound outward, the weather didn't seem to hold much promise for us. It had been blowing from the north-east for some time, but looked like a change and so our first stop would be back down the river at Grays. After a couple of days there the wind backed to the north and 'Tintack' agreed that we should jog down to Southend and get a few fish.

Heaving short, the wind was still gusting out of the north, so we only prepared the foresail as far as headsails went, and set a full mainsail and topsail.

Her cargo aboard, the *Saltcote Belle* awaits her tide and a fair wind.

We held the foresail aback to windward to break the anchor out and let her lie until we had got the anchor right home. Then it was let draw and away we went with more than just a steady breeze. 'Tintack' and I were, as usual, in cracking form when we were off like that!

We had just entered the top of Gravesend Reach and I had passed comment to 'Tintack' that we would have to watch out for any heavy squalls. He had just gone forward to pull the fo'c'sle hatch closed, as we had spray coming aboard, when I heard a loud crack which turned into a splintering crash. I shouted to 'Tintack' to jump as the topmast came crashing down. On a sailing barge that meant down below, not over the side!

I threw the barge round on the other tack. We left the foresail on the bowline and hove half the mainsail up so the barge then lay hove to, making no way forward, and with just the tide soaking us down the reach. That was an occasion when having an expert mate was a great help and between us we were soon hacking into this and that to clear the mess. The remains of the topmast were lashed in the lee scuppers and the topsail was hurled on the fore hatch. Anything that we could throw into the fo'c'sle went down there. 'Tintack' went down to restore some sort of order later on. After we got the worst cleared away I asked 'Tintack' if he thought we should carry on. 'Yes, why not?' he said and so we decided to keep going, rigged like a stumpy[1]. We still managed to get down to Southend and joined a few others that lay there, tucking ourselves well in. But alas, no fish. I couldn't believe it. Next day it was still the same, so I got into our boat and making fast our dolly wire I went off as far as the wire would let me, about two hundred yards. I then let go the dinghy's anchor and as soon as I got my gear down on the bottom I was into the fish.

After three hours fishing 'Tintack' decided he was ready for dinner. As he hove me back on the dolly wire I pulled up the dinghy anchor and was soon alongside. Later, whilst 'Tintack' gutted my catch, I stayed below trying to get some warmth into myself. During the second night our motion had changed and I took a look at the glass which showed quite a rise. Looking at our bob, the wind had shifted to the east-north-east and was blowing much harder.

On the first of the daylight we hove short, and with just a couple of cloths of the mainsail we broke out the anchor with the foresail to windward. We were soon on our way back, not a way we liked going, but it would have taken too long and been too wet to go for Sheerness. We were going back up, to Holehaven Creek, and after a nice easy sail we were able to find a good berth, just off the jetty that led up to the pub, the Lobster Smack. We lived off our fish for the couple of days we stayed there.

Some of the other barges went right back up to the Lower Hope. I think most of them didn't like a pint. The old Lobster Smack sold good beer, and good chicken eggs. A few sweepings from us meant a few beers, and so we were able to really enjoy our stay.

---

[1] A 'stumpy' barge was one that set no topsail and carried no topmast. They tended to occupy the shorter river trades, where sailing performance was not critical. The topsail barge which dominated the coasting trades was a development of the 'stumpy'.

At last our slant came, but only from the south-east, and we hove short but prepared to wait for the tide to come away to get out of the creek. I had started to fume a bit for I would need all of the ebb with just our stumpy rig. But lady luck was with us, for the old rubbish barge tug appear from up the creek towing his empty, but still smelly, 'rough stuff' lighters. He gave a turn to one of the craft that was inside us, and as they passed close to us shouted, 'Pass your line' so we were much earlier away.

We headed down about an hour before high water and with a good force five we had plenty enough to stem the last of the flood tide, and were making good speed. We had a nice uneventful sail down to and through the Spitway then squared away up for the Knoll and on into the River Colne. We made it up to the moorings in Marriage's Bight, to lie ready for the tow up next day.

Towing up the last of the Colne went smoothly. 'Tintack' cleared the hatches of ropes and lashings and got as much ready as he could for our discharge. At Colchester the motor boat towed us right up as far as he could to Hythe Bridge where we moored to prepare to lower our gear down so we could tackle the remainder of our run up to East Mills.

As soon as we had tied up, our 'Governor', Mr Josh Francis, came out of the office and gave me a piece of his mind about losing a topmast. He then tried to explain to me about some barges being tender and others stiff, and that's why some topsails you had to drop whilst others you could carry. I then shut him up with a cheeky, 'Well I've learnt that for myself now, haven't I?' He just turned on his heels and went back into his office.

We had at least three days to lie down at the quay before we would have enough water to attempt to get up to the mills. That time was put to good use cleaning up our damaged gear. The topsail was sent over to Taylors at Maldon for repair, and we were also able to ship a new topmast. We were told that the topsail would be ready for us when we got back down to the quay, so we could bend it on before we hove up our gear.

The main work for us then was to get the barge ready for our trip up through the bridges. First we had to uncover part of the main hatchway near the mastcase, and then on the centre line dig a short run fore and aft in the cargo. There was a piece of headledge[1] that we could take out, enabling the mast to be lowered into the trench. The rudder was put in the midships position and the king spoke, which was the one that has the brass knob on it, and also has a bolt going through the hub, was removed. The wheel could not be used after that had been done.

As soon as we floated on the up-going tide, we stood by until all our mooring ropes were off. When we felt her move we pushed for all we were worth with the long setting booms, punting the old *Saltcote Belle* all the way from the Hythe up to the East Mills, at the bottom of Colchester's East Hill. It was a hard and long haul, but our exertions were not over, for after we had

---

[1] The timbers which project up from the deck to form the hatchway are called headledges fore and aft of the opening to the hold; the sides of the hatchways known as coamings.

arrived and moored, we had to heave the gear up again so the elevator could get into the hold and discharge us. That involved us turning out on the night tides to pull the barge ahead or astern, to allow the elevator a new position for its next day's work. Discharging that way would often take three days. When empty and going back down, we had to first lower the gear flat as before. As soon as the ebb tide allowed our stem blocks to go beneath the mill bridge, we had to go like the clappers. Each of us with one of the old setting booms buried into our shoulders, we worked furiously, quanting the barge down until we reached Hythe Quay, and before we touched ground.

Moored back at the quay again, our topsail was delivered, and 'Tintack' and I soon had us fully rigged. I thought that with our delays because of the topmast and the topsail repair, it could be said that we'd been 'on the yard',

Ivan's name appears as Master on this six-monthly return completed a few weeks after taking the *Saltcote Belle*.

and so would take first priority for next orders. Going into the office with that view in mind, it was soon to be changed, for we had one hell of a row. A craft that had unloaded after us was to load grit, which I said should have been our cargo. They said they didn't think we would be ready in time to load, but they had not asked us.

After that I came to look upon some at our firm's office as having their favourites, and I certainly was not one of them. I think it was because I spoke my mind with regard to various things I had issues with. I told them the mate and I were both looking elsewhere and they would be hearing from us in the near future.

Having decided the way we both felt we decided to go home for a couple of days. The only order they could give us was London empty and nothing in the offing. I said to 'Tintack' that the way it was blowing we were best alongside the quay, and so we lay for four days. We were at home during that time spending a few bob and looking around, but everyone had the same tales of woe to tell, so we just had to grin and bear it.

Back at Colchester there was still nothing doing. We decided to go to London, although it was still blowing from the south-west about a force five. After the motor boat had dropped us and we were making our way out of the Colne, I said to 'Tintack' that we wouldn't be going very far that day. It was blowing quite hard out clear of the land, so I decided that we would try and push up through the Ray Sand Channel towards the Shore Ends at the entrance to the River Crouch. I knew that I could run back to the Colne if the going got too bad for us. Again we were lucky and managed to get through, there to meet up with an old friend, the *Gladys*, belonging to Shrubsalls.

Looking out at times during the night showed nothing to suggest that we would be underway the next day. By breakfast next morning the wind had changed. I said to 'Tintack' that we would get underway a couple of hours before the high water and try to make a passage. The breeze had gone southerly, so I thought that we could go over the top of the sands and then as the ebb came away it would help to set us off from the sand and push us to windward. 'Tintack' agreed that we give it a go. Getting underway was no easy job for we were bucking and rearing. It made for a very long and laborious heave. We had to watch ourselves as the old girl set back and snatched on the windlass handles, and we could have received a nasty clout or worse.

Gladys was a popular name for a barge, the four best known conveniently with different Ports of Registry. Shrubsall's *Gladys* was registered at Dover, built at Sandwich in 1900.

After getting ourselves away the *Gladys* decided to follow but she was no match for us. We were away with just the topsail sheet, full mainsail and the foresail, and what a trip it turned out to be. We had made the late afternoon high water around the Shoebury jetty and it was really black all around. I said to 'Tintack' that we were in for a very rough night, but I will say the old *'Belle'* didn't let us down. I made a board right across to the Kentish shore on the high water slack and I was able to work us up to the top of the Swatchway. Once into about three fathoms of water we were in a good position to bring up, so as I roared us round through the wind 'Tintack' dropped the foresail down. Then it was let go the anchor and feed her about twenty fathoms of chain, after which we knew she would lie okay.

Whilst I set about doing the final stow 'Tintack' was putting the kettle on and going to prepare a bit of grub. He came flying up on deck again saying that he thought that we could be sinking. I just laughed and said I reckoned that the kettle had spilled and gone over the floor, but on looking below I knew that 'Tintack' could be right. The two pumps were shipped aft and we had a very long spell pumping before we had the water below the cabin floor and we called it a day. We felt better once we got stuck in to plenty of tea and soon had the old pan on. The bacon, eggs and beans really tasted good. After we had cleared the lot and washed up, the water was still beneath the cabin floor, so I said, 'Right, mate, we'll turn in and see what the morning brings.'

Our trip up river from there on in had to be done very carefully. The wind had fallen light to moderate, but we decided not to set the topsail so as not to over press her. I had decided to go to Grays on the next flood and hire a petrol engine powered pump to see if we could get rid of our water. We seemed all right on our run up the river. I went ashore to Goldsmith's yard and they said I could borrow a pump for no charge, as long as I returned it that same day, and put my own petrol in. Once back on board we were soon set up and pumping. In the space of a couple of hours we reckoned that we were dry. We then pulled up a few limber boards[1] and had a good clean right through the holds. By just keeping the hatches off we dried out fairly well, and each day of our stay we did the same thing until we felt that we could load cargo once again.

The old 'Belle' never made water like that again, and we could only think that it was because she was 'hog-backed'. She had made plenty of water to tell us she didn't like being given a pasting when she was empty. We hadn't cause to do it again. We lay at Grays for nearly a couple of weeks. I had been told that there were still five on turn ahead of us at the Woolwich 'Starvation Buoys', so we thought we would stay where we were. Although I was ringing both morning and afternoon, we still couldn't get a job. Quite a lot of the Goldsmith fleet were lying with us, also awaiting orders. They had a lot more chance of getting work for they had a lot of local connections for the river trades as well as coasting, so we didn't hold out much hope for a quick shift from there.

Halfway through the second week 'Tintack' and I were both thinking that it was time to up anchor and go back to Colchester to jack it in. I think he more or less convinced me we should take a freight down with us, so as to get some money. So we decided we should stick it out to the end of the second week and see what would happen. I went ashore in the afternoon but we received no orders, and I told our London broker that we would probably be going back to Colchester at the end of the week, tying her up and finishing. I said I would ring up and let him know before we did anything about going down the river.

In the mornings we went ashore at ten-thirty, when I would ring up to see if there was anything doing. Then we would usually go and have a pint and a chat with the lads.

---

[1] Removeable boards in the ceiling (hold floor) giving access to the limber holes, cut to allow bilge water to flow through the transverse floor timbers to the pumps.

The next morning turned into something different. When I got through to the London office they said we could go to Ipswich to pick up a cargo of timber from Cliff Quay, to be carried to Heybridge Basin for discharge. When I asked about the craft at Woolwich buoys, he said they wouldn't go, and so I had no need to worry about sailing for turn, at least amongst our own craft.

We strolled up the road and just got ourselves a couple of loaves of bread and little else, and then we were off back on board. I said to 'Tintack' that it was his chance to have a go. He could give the orders and I'd be the mate, for he was always saying be might like to go Skipper one day.

He got one thing wrong straight away, for he gave me the order to heave short and he had forgotten to lift the boat into the davits. With a grunt he just said, 'I forgot.' Getting underway with 'Tintack' was really no different than it would have been with me, except it was a little confusing taking the orders instead of giving them. All the way down I think he made the right decisions, although his memory for compass courses and buoy names left a lot of room for improvement!

'Tintack' at the wheel and issuing the orders, whilst Ivan does the mate's job.

As we approached the Swin Spitway buoy there was the motor barge *Atrato* gilling about waiting for water over. Her skipper was a good friend of mine and I gave him a cheery wave as we sailed straight by him. With our two foot, nine inch draught we were able to leave him a few miles astern, managing to keep ahead of him until he caught up with us at Shotley. He then told me to stow up, came alongside and pulled us right up to our ship at Cliff Quay. Only when he was sure that we were all right did he leave us and proceed himself to the dock for locking in. He was bound right up into the top corner of the dock, to Cranfields Flour Mills to discharge his grain cargo. He was then coming out to load timber from the same ship as us, but bound for the Medway to a wharf near Rochester Bridge.

Fred and the *Atrato* were out and alongside our ship before we got our cargo, so we both sort of loaded together. As we were being filled by Ipswich dockers there was no need for us to get into the hold. They made a very good stow of any cargo, so 'Tintack' and I could sort out the chains and wires that we needed for our cargo lashings. As we neared completion Fred said that if we could be ready for six in the morning he would give us a start down. 'Tintack' and I worked through that evening to make sure that all the lashings were in place and that we were ready to go.

At six next morning Fred slid the *Atrato* alongside us as promised. He said that he would tie us alongside and drop us in Harwich harbour. We let go from the ship and were on our way a little after six, a half ebb leave. The wind was a steady force three to four from the north-east and Fred said that we

The motor barge *Atrato* was built of steel in 1898 as a sailorman, but was converted to fully powered when just 25 years old. Ipswich skipper Fred Smy was in her during Ivan's time in barges.

would be going up the Wallet a lot more comfortably than he would, and he was right. As soon as we were off the Naze we found that there was a very heavy swell running. It was about low water, and the wind over tide had created conditions left us really rolling along, and at speed, for the conditions suited the old *Saltcote Belle*.

Whilst the *Atrato* wallowed and rolled, our run was as pleasant as we could have wished or expected, our sails giving us a much steadier trip. Our timber stack seemed to be acting as an additional sail and I said to 'Tintack' that we would be up to Heybridge Basin in very good time. As we came up around the west side of Osea Island towards the Doctor buoy, where the water starts to shoal, we stowed up leaving just enough sail set to keep control of the old girl. When we approached the gutway towards the lock pit we got rid of the last of our sail, and came to a halt in the mud just before we got to and hit the gate!

After we had tied up in the dock 'Tintack' and I had very little to do, except to go to the pub and drink beer. As we had just had such a good sail, all thoughts of leaving went out of our minds once again - until the next bad time.

132 Having discharged our cargo I decided that we would lie at Heybridge until we had definite orders. It was a very pleasant place to stay and the costs were zero. There was nothing doing our end or in London. In any case our firm had craft in London that were on turn before us. We had a week's lie before we started to get itchy feet again. After about ten days our office rang the pub one lunch time and gave us orders for Millwall Docks to load a cargo of maize for Ipswich. They didn't want us for another four days so I thought we would have another night in the Jolly Sailor, and leave on the next day's tide.

I took the opportunity to give them my notice, and they asked if I would sail the *Saltcote Belle* back to Colchester from Ipswich on yard pay, if they couldn't find a relief for me. Then they asked if I thought that the mate was competent enough to take her, and I said he was. I was to put it to him and to ring them back with his answer, so they would know whether they had to advertise the berth.

I put their proposition to 'Tintack', but he said a no with a capital N, and then asked if I would ring them up again and tell them he would be leaving as well. I had felt that was what he might say, as his opinion was like mine. We were getting less and less orders and a lot more waiting about, and although we were just able to scratch a living it was getting to be quite a struggle.

Locking out of the basin the next day, my thoughts turned to the times 'Tintack' and I had spent aboard the *'Belle'*, and we both agreed that we would miss the sailing lark, but we were looking forward to going into power. After a little bit of reminiscing we buckled down to the job in hand, thinking how to get the best out of the old girl and get her to London. When we started we were blessed with a breeze in the right direction, but as we entered the Lower Hope the wind started to die on us and by the time we were going up Gravesend Reach it had given up altogether.

When off the World's End, just below Tilbury, I had to let go the anchor for fear of driving on to the landing stage. We looked like spending the night there, but it was not a place where you could go to sleep in comfort. I was relieved when next morning we were able to pick up a breeze and get out of it. We managed to reach the dock entrance on the tide.

Once we were in the dock we were given confirmation of when we were going to load. It was as we had been told before we had left Heybridge, and we still had two full days to lie. So 'Tintack' came up to the city with me, as he'd never been there before, and we made a day of it. One night we had quite a good time at the old Queen's Theatre just outside the docks, and of course a few beers, so our stay in the dock seemed to pass quickly by!

Loading at the Central Granary took only an hour, the cargo being just one hundred tons. With less than a full hold we looked forward to a reasonably fast passage. But alas, lady luck was not to be with us on that trip.

Coming out of the dock we were soon to find that the visibility was no good. With the little wind that we had, I said to 'Tintack' that we should find a decent set of lighter roads to lie on until the fog cleared a bit. And so it was we came to stay on Tate and Lyle's roads for three days, and there was no movement on the river during that time. The craft had no electronic aids in those days, and I don't remember seeing anything with radar unless it belonged to the Navy or Customs. After three days we were able to have another little sail and managed to get down just below Gravesend to the Denton anchorage, and there to tuck ourselves in out of the big ships' way.

The Millwall Dock Central Granary was easy to spot, towering over the surrounding buildings.

It seemed to me that ships always wanted to chase a barge wherever they lay, or even if they were underway. Even in those days, when we were under sail, many of the ships didn't understand what a sailing barge was doing, so there were always plenty of close calls and occasionally a collision.

Another couple of days were to pass before we were able to proceed any further on account of

The Denton anchorage was a spot where barges could bring up clear of shipping in poor visibility.

that frustrating bloody fog, and we kept muttering, 'So much for our fast and easy run.' Eventually we got just a sniff of a very light wind from the south-east and we hove up feeling a lot better, but still the fog hung about. We ghosted a bit further and finished up on the low water, just to the north and east of the wartime wreck of the Liberty Ship, the *Richard Montgomery* which lies in the Swatchway just outside Sheerness. It lies there loaded full of explosives, so all ships give it a very wide berth. We knew we were fairly safe, so we went below again for our tea and eats, and after a smoke and a yarn it was onto the locker for a couple of hours' rest.

I had set the alarm clock for midnight, as it was our intention to get underway then. As often seemed to be the case, we were on the go before the alarm went off and I soon had the kettle boiled and the brew going. As we finished our smoke I said to 'Tintack' that I hoped to get us over into the Swin that tide, and thought we might get a tow from one of the sand barges down the Swin if only we could get there. I noticed that the lights of the shipping around us were reflected from the heavy moisture in the air. I said to Tintack that I hoped it was not going to close right in again. I think we kidded each other that it wasn't too bad as we both wanted to get home, having loaded our final cargo.

We hove short the anchor and got the mainsail and topsail set, but there wasn't enough wind to fill them out. We then set the staysail as a headsail and hove the anchor right up, saying that we wouldn't cat it in case we had to let it go again in a hurry. Then I had a word to 'Tintack' to ensure that he keep his eyes and ears open. I was even blowing our old hand foghorn, although I doubt many would have heard it from far away.

'Tintack' was pacing up and down the weather deck and going for'ard. At about the same time as I heard it, he reported that he could hear a ship's engine, much too close for comfort.

I am convinced to this day that this ship was not blowing, but even if he had been we still couldn't have done anything to avoid what followed. We had lost the wind and as we were lying more or less athwart the tide on our drift down with the tide, there was no telling what might happen. I told 'Tintack' to be ready to jump below if I had cause to shout out, and that I would do the same if he yelled.

The next thing was the sight of a port light high up on this passing ship, the stern of which sort of dragged across our bows. 'Tintack' shouted and so did I, so he went down the fo'c'sle and I went down the cabin in a hurry. The crunch of the collision didn't seem too bad and within a couple of minutes I had sort of recovered and I nipped forward to make sure 'Tintack' was okay. Then I just let go the anchor to bring us head up into the tide. The ship was also letting go its anchor and I clearly heard the four bells to denote sixty fathoms had been let go. The next hour went by very fast. A quick look-see showed us that we were not leaking badly through the stem, but some was coming through the bolts that held the stem apron in place. We quickly prepared and drove in some softwood kindling plugs around the bolts, and in time those were to swell and keep most of the water out.

The ship had been shouting down to us through their megaphone and, as I answered them, they suggested sending a lifebelt down on a line to give us a wire. As they lay just up tide of us it was easily done. Once I spotted the belt I just gave the barge a sheer and 'Tintack' was able to get it with a boathook. We pulled on the belt's line and shortly got the end of the wire which was passed through the hawse eye on the starboard bow and then hooked over the bow cleat. The ship then took the strain and we were slowly able to get our anchor in and were hove up alongside. The ship had plenty of fenders over and using their ropes we could say we were fairly snug whilst it stayed fine.

The First Mate of the ship came down aboard us, mainly I think to assess the damage to his ship, but their paint wasn't even marked. I then showed him our damage, but he was really out of his depth aboard us. When I explained about the hand pumping he got two ABs to come down off the ship to take care of it. He said that the Master and the Pilot would like to see me on board as soon as I was able. Before 'Tintack' and I boarded the ship we had one more check down the fo'c'sle and, as we couldn't hear or see anything coming in, I told the ABs to go down into the cabin in the warm and to try the pumps about every half hour we were away. I gave 'Tintack' instructions to say nothing and we slowly made our way up the ship's side on their Jacob's ladder. The lad at the top escorted us to the Master's cabin, and a proper kingdom it was too. It seemed to us as though the Captain had the very best of everything. The Master and the Pilot seemed to have knocked a few gins back whilst they had been waiting for us to appear.

The Mate had given the Master his report, and I think he was just keen to get our side of the story. All I said was that if the ship hadn't have gone hard to starboard, I'm sure we would have gone clear. The Pilot more or less agreed with me. At the time of the incident the Master was on the bridge as well as the Third Mate and the Pilot. It was the Third Mate who had seen us at the last minute and as a natural reaction had shouted, 'Hard a starboard' and in so doing had caused the stern of the ship to give us this clout.

Going back down the Jacob's to get back on board had to be done very carefully, for as well as our stomachs having a few gins in them, we had each a bottle and a couple of hundred fags, so we were in good spirits. We shared a couple of glasses with the two ABs and then sent them off aboard their ship. On our last try at the pumps we couldn't get any water at all. After a couple of hours below the Mate of the ship was back on board, as by then it was daylight, to have a further check round.

The Mate said that the Master wanted to know if there was anything that they could do for us. After a quick word with 'Tintack' I asked if they could give us a tow up off Holehaven Creek. As there was a faint breeze we could perhaps sail onto the mud and have a good check around before we went any further.

As all the Mate had to do was to convince the Master, he agreed, saying that there would be no problem, and so we were duly slacked astern of the ship on their wire. They were very good, towing us at about four knots. By the time we were up off the creek we could see that there was very little water in there, and so the ship dropped us just below it. As it was flood tide we just nicely fetched into the creek and into a good berth.

We had a thorough look around again and I decided that we should drive more wooden plugs alongside the bolts in the stem apron, and then attempt to encase the damaged area in pitch.. In our fo'c'sle store we found the best parts of some old hatch cloths which we nailed over the damage with battens, making a sort of canvas funnel with the opening at the top. 'Tintack', in the meantime, had broken up a load of our pitch, something wooden barges always carried, and melted it in our cast iron two-gallon boiling pot. As soon as the first lot was liquid it was poured down the funnel until we were satisfied that it had got into all the bolt holes and any other damaged parts before it set. We then added more until our canvas 'funnel' was full. At the end of it we thought we had done a very good job.

The next thing I had to do was to let the office know what had happened. I had already written a report out so it just remained for me to make the phone call, to post the report, have a pint and then get back on board and get cracking.

Returning to the *'Belle'* we hove up the boat into the davits and then the anchor, and we were on our way once more with a steady breeze from the southward, and hopes for a reasonable trip. In those days before VHF radios you had to be your own best judge of weather, and that trip I got it all wrong. The barometer hadn't shown much change but, with the amount of fog and fine weather we had enjoyed, I should have known that when it did change that it would blow.

It turned out to be change with a vengeance! We had left with just a gentle breeze but by the time we had got to the Blacktail Spit, we had more than enough wind. I said to 'Tintack' that there was no way we were going round the outside of the Gunfleet in our state and eventually we found ourselves having to anchor at the Spitway. 'Tintack' was already having to pump nearly all the time, so our prospects didn't look too good, and it was getting worse as we lay there. One motor barge came to us to see if we were all right, and, as the pumping was keeping pace with the leaks at that time, we waved him on his way.

About another hour was to pass before I began to realise the serious situation that we were in. After a quick word with 'Tintack' I made my mind up what must be done. I decided to fire off one of our rockets, but received no reply. On firing another a little later I got an answer, not from Clacton just three miles from the lifeboat, but from a yacht nearly as big as the *Saltcote Belle*, with twin screws and all sorts of gear. He came as fast as he could but had to ease down owing to the swell that had built up where we were anchored. 'Tintack' had stowed the topsail whilst I had sent the rocket up, and then we pitched the second anchor over, putting the riding light up and the stern light in place. We collected our wallets from below and battened the cabin and fo'c'sle down and also the cabin skylight. We were then ready to leave her.

The motor yacht was nearly up to us by the time all that was done, and although it was then well dark, I felt sure we had done all we could to make her safe. We were confident that when we left her, she couldn't be just picked up by others. The large motor yacht came just to windward of us but there was no way we could leap across.

After he had also tried the lee side I realised that he wasn't going to be able to get close enough for us to jump. I shouted that we would get into our dinghy if they could get a line over to us, and then we would drop clear. They hadn't got a good heaving line, so I stood in the head of our dinghy whilst it was still in the davits to throw our line over. On the second throw they managed to catch it with their boathook and they kept station just to windward of us like a lifeboat. When 'Tintack' and I lowered the boat we both had to get it just right. As we hit the water I had to look sharp with the line and just got a turn on the forward hook in the boat, although doing all that in oilskins and bulky lifejackets was very awkward.

The yacht had very good searchlights and also a first-class Skipper. He just held her head into the weather and we were able to pull ourselves up under his stern, which gave us a good lee enabling us to climb up his boarding ladder. Taking our painters we made the boat fast on his stern.

Going into the wheelhouse was like going into a greenhouse. It was very hot, especially for us with all our heavy weather gear, which we were soon invited to remove. After a short chat the Skipper decided that we could go into Brightlingsea, provided that I could assist him as he was more or less on his own. The wheelhouse was fairly full of ladies and a few Hooray Henrys, but all in all they were a very likeable lot.

The Skipper offered me the wheel, and I asked them to mind their glasses as we would be turning to put the swell on the port beam and then shaping to go through the Spitway. One of them noticed that we hadn't got a glass but that was soon put right. Tintack was quite at home with the ladies, and there was quite a lot of old chat going on. I think some of them had had more than enough to drink.

Soon after we had passed through the Spitway the Walton lifeboat, which was on its way to us, had received a recall. The lifeboat's radio operator had been chatting to our yacht as we had come over the Spitway, so they knew that everything was all right and the crew of the barge were safe.

Somewhere between the Swin Spitway buoy and the Inner Bench Head our boat was lost. Perhaps it was a good job we didn't see it go, or we may have made an attempt to get it and added to our troubles.

Slowly, we approached the creek mouth in the darkness, and at last we made out the leading lights into the creek and made our way up to the hard area. One of the local fishermen put us onto a buoy just inside the approach to Cindy Island. Bidding our farewells and thanks, 'Tintack' and I were taken ashore to the Anchor Inn at the top of the hard. Whilst there we were given a few pints and shorts, then the lady from the Shipwrecked Mariners Society arrived to help us. As I was a paid up member, the landlord had rung them up for me. We were taken to a café in the town and there given a huge meal and a good bed each. Our clothes were taken away, and in the morning we were called with a cup of tea, and all our gear had been washed, dried out and pressed up.

The Anchor was a welcome haven for Ivan and 'Tintack', having abandoned the *Saltcote Belle* at the Spitway.

Going down stairs brought another surprise, as a smashing breakfast had been cooked for us. As much as we could eat and all the coffee and tea we could drink was to be had for the asking. As we said our thank-yous before we left, we were asked where we were going. I realised we didn't really know. The lady at the café suggested that I rang around to see what could be sorted, so there was more coffee as I made my list.

After sitting down with a piece of paper, I decided that the first call to be made was to the Coastguards, who informed me that the old girl was still where we had left her. They also said that looking seawards the main swell had gone, and the wind was force six from the north-west, so things had changed for the better.

Next I phoned Mr Josh to put him in the picture and suggested that we try to get back on board. After a bit of mumbling he agreed that was about all we could do, but he wanted to know how would we do it. I said I'd let him know something later, and it was to be much later!

I first found two powered smacks which were prepared to have a go. As they came down the river from Wivenhoe, one of them came into Brightlingsea Creek and picked up 'Tintack' and me. Just before we left I rang the Coastguards again and told them of our intentions. When they asked where I thought we would end up; I said Davy Jones' Locker or, more hopefully, somewhere up the Crouch.

As we approached the Wallet Spitway I could see we were not going to have it easy. I said to the smack Skipper that once we were on board I would check on the water situation before we decided if the old 'Belle' was fit to have a go. If it was not too bad we would slip both anchors for the smacks to recover and, with the wind the way it was, we would then go on our way up to Burnham.

We still had a bit of a lee from the Buxey Sands, but the smack had a hell of a job to get us anywhere near the barge. I think both 'Tintack' and myself jumped much before it was safe to do so. Any rate, once aboard, we could see the poor old girl was in a bit of a state and very low in the water. Being loaded with only one hundred tons saved her, I'm sure. Once I had assessed the situation I decided that we would pump as we sailed.

We spent a little time cutting a lump off our dolly wire to make fast to the main anchor chain to which we attached a marker buoy. We did the same to the second anchor wire, and with the mainsail set and sheeted home and the foresail drawing we slipped the anchor chain over the side, followed by the wire. We were on our own, with the smacks standing by. One moved in fast and picked the wire up and so recovered our second anchor, but they hadn't time to attempt the main anchor cable.After the second smack caught up with us again her Skipper thought we might be able to take the anchor back on board while we were sailing up the Whitaker Channel. But there was no way we could attempt it for not only was there still quite a swell rolling us along, but I was doing the sailing and 'Tintack' was full time doing the pumping. We were much too busy to do anything else until we closed the land and found more shelter.

Water was flowing about freely down below, and 'Tintack' even thought that we were possibly making more as we sailed. We had one smack to windward and the other to leeward, and our cumbersome lifejackets on, so with luck we should have been able to save ourselves should the old girl succumb. At times, in some of the squalls, the smacks had a job to keep up. With the flood tide beneath us and the wind about six, the 'Belle' was really giving her best. It seemed as if she was telling us that she wasn't done yet.

As we closed the land, I thought we were starting to sag to leeward more, and so I made up my mind that we should have one of the smacks tow us the last few miles to Priors of Burnham. We had one ahead of us and the other on our lee quarter. 'Tintack' and I were able to give ourselves a smart harbour stow for all the sails. Priors gave us a good berth on their yard, and left us alone for a few hours after we had tied up.

I wrote a couple of 'receipts' for the two smacks as to what they had done. They both stayed the night alongside us for they were going off the next day to have a go for the main anchor and cable. I learnt in due course that somebody beat them to it, for although they dragged for it nothing was ever found. They later took the 'receipts' into our Colchester Office and were duly paid for their services. I know that one got sixty pounds for recovery and returning our second anchor and cable, but I don't know what they got for putting us back aboard and the trip standing by.

In the very early morning next day Priors were over the port side on the mud, and using a power tool soon had a few large holes drilled along the chine. When we turned out a little later, the water was pouring out of these holes, and before the low water there was just a dribble from each hole. One of the shipwrights and a lad then came along and drove wooden trunnels into these holes, and I said to 'Tintack' that we should be able to forget the pumps.

I informed our office that we were ready to go somewhere to unload. It had been suggested that our wetted cargo wouldn't have been much good for anything, and so they were looking for someone else to take it off Paul's hands. Our firm had been doing something about it, for they came up with a new discharge port; Hullbridge, just up the river from where we were lying.

A couple of days were to pass before the tides were right for us to go up to Hullbridge. I had met and chatted to the old huffler in the pub, so I had a good idea that we were in for a bit of tricky work, but anything different we used to treat as a new challenge. Casting off from Priors was a little nerve-racking as there were craft all around us, but they shoved a few out of the way and we were able to find a route to sail through those they left. Once we were clear the huffler took the wheel. As the river narrowed, there still looked to be plenty of water about, but most of it was just covering up the mudflats either side of the twisting channel.

When we arrived off the Hullbridge jetty, the idea was to let go our remaining anchor and swing to it, and then to put a line ashore and heave alongside the so-called wharf, paying out our second anchor wire as we closed the jetty. That all went very well, except that once alongside, the second anchor should have been the one to go out aft, but in our case it had to be just our small kedge. As the jetty was small - only about twenty feet long, our springs were short and the breast ropes had to go to suitable trees. Once there, all was sort of hove tight to the huffler's satisfaction. The old fellow then took his leave with

Looking east at Burnham-on-Crouch, the large building beyond and to the left of the yacht-barge is Prior's yard, their crane on the wharfside where vessels would lie when in for repair.

the parting shot, 'See you when you're empty, and don't forget my chickens,' so his bag had to be amongst our sweepings.

After we had enjoyed a good meal our thoughts turned to the shore side. We knew nothing about the place. As soon as we were nicely spruced up we were off, but I'm afraid we were in for a shock for there didn't seem to be any life at all in the place. The natural choice was a pub, and the best we could find was the one that was just off the quayside where we lay.

We were made to feel very much at home there, and were even better off when they knew what our cargo was. Once we had sorted out the rewards for our sweepings, we knew that we would be all right for beer money and fresh eggs. We settled into a nice routine and thoroughly enjoyed our stay with these folk.

Two days were to pass before we were contacted by the farmer who had purchased the cargo. It was agreed that 'Tintack' and I would assist in the unloading for a rate of sixpence ($2^1/_2$p) a ton. So for our one hundred tons we were to receive two pounds and ten shillings (£2.50) each for our work. The farmer had a two-wheel cart and a lovely old horse to pull it. First we had to get the barge ready and that meant the gin wheel had to be pulled aloft on the topsail halyard and the topsail sheet. The sprit was set up to plumb the cart, and a guy line was set up to hold the basket off. That was taken to a cleat on the offside coaming. Then the heaving wire was taken around the mastcase winch. The idea was that the basket would be filled down in the hold by a couple of the farm hands. 'Tintack' would then heave the basket out of the hold while I kept the weight on the guy. As soon as the basket was at cart height I would let the guy off sharply, and check it when it reached over the cart. Once it was tipped into the cart I would pull the empty basket back again and 'Tintack' would slack it down into the hold as before. Many a cart load and much hoisting and swinging of the basket went on until after nearly five days, we saw the last of the cargo go out. We took up the limber boards and gave the hold and bilge a really good clean out. As we had finished with the *'Belle'* we lay there a couple more days to really give her a chance to dry out. We had to get rid of the last of the sweepings of course, and have a few more beers in return.

Once again we were all ready to go and I said to 'Tintack' on our third morning after discharge, 'Right, mate, this is our day.' Trying to contact the huffler, his good lady told me that he had got one to take up to Battlesbridge, so wouldn't be able to take us down. I told Tintack, 'We'll go on our own, mate.' He just grinned and said, 'Right, mate.' I asked if he wanted to be Skipper for the, trip but he said no.

I couldn't really remember where the water lay, and I said that with the fair wind, as soon as we floated we'd go. We let go everything from the shore, and then as soon as we moved we got the kedge and second anchor aboard. With the staysail and topsail we left the quayside very sedately. As soon as we could, we powered on the mainsail and were well away on our last trip.

Our westerly wind held until we were nearly off East Mersea Island Point, when it fell flat, so we had to bring up. The ballastmen which went up the Colne to load would already have been up past so we wouldn't have a chance to get up to the moorings without a breeze. 'Tintack' and I had plenty of

Prior's 'ballastmen' go from the Colne to the London River with timetable regularity in all weathers. The Beaufort Scale describes these conditions as 'Violent Storm'.

time for reminiscing that evening, and the subject came up as to what we were going to do in the future. 'I think I'll join the army.' he suggested, and I said, 'Oh yeah! I think I might try for the Marines.'

Next day dawned very fine with hardly any wind at all, but as the flood tide made in, we got underway and sort of drifted towards Freshwater Jetty just above Alresford. I thought we might have to anchor again, but over the horizon we could hear the heavy throb of a diesel engine and knew that one of Prior's sandmen was about. We had high hopes of a lug up just through Marriages Bight. As he came up to us he just took our line and soon we were flying along. As we got up to the sandman's berth the little motor-boat from Colchester took our rope, and so we continued uninterrupted all the way to Hythe Quay.

As soon as we moored I went into our office to let them know we had arrived. I drew the freight money, so 'Tintack' and I became loaded again. We decided that we were not going home until the Friday morning and would get stuck into a bit of work.

After the shipwrights had assessed the extent of the damage it was decided that they would have to take the stem apron piece off to make repairs. That meant we would have to release the stem block that carried the stayfall that held up the mast, to let them start work. We lowered the topmast and then put a very heavy chain around the mainmast head. The rolling vang tackles were attached to each end of the chain and down onto the bows, set tight and made fast on the bow cleats each side. We were then able to slack everything away so the lower stem block could be removed, and left the rest up to the shipwright and his boy.

They set a raft about the bow so they could work when the tide was in, with the trestles and boards in the raft with them so they could also work on the low water. All the damaged timber and our temporary repair was pulled away and the bolts were drawn out. A blacksmith was given the job to sort out the fastenings.

It didn't take long for the tradesmen to do their jobs. It was more of a question of waiting for materials. A couple of days after receiving his oak, and the bolts, the shipwright had declared the job finished. The raft was left so that we could get plenty of tar around the area of the repair outside. All that was left for 'Tintack' and me to do was to re-rig the stem blocks and forestay. That only gave us a day's work, and then I was able to go into the office and draw my eight pounds yard pay, and 'Tintack's' five pounds for sailing light from Hullbridge to Colchester and about ten days' work on the quay. So we were paid off not broke, but badly bent, and both intending to go our separate ways.

144 'Tintack' and I had had a couple of days at home and we were lost as to what to do. We were seeing each other for a beer at lunch times and again in the evenings if we hadn't a date. We both knew that we couldn't keep that up for long as we had nothing coming in. One morning 'Tintack' and I were at the recruitment office at ten o'clock, he to try and join the army and myself to try for the marine commandos. I passed most of the stuff to get in, and then came the bad news that they would have to reject me as I was just half an inch too short. They told me to push myself the extra bit and then go back. I just said, 'Sorry mate, if not this time, never. I'll go back to sea.' My old mate 'Tintack' somehow bluffed his way through the eyesight test, although one of his eyes was nearly useless. He got into the army, only to get kicked out again after just eighty-four days.

So we really had gone our separate ways and I felt a lot more settled in myself and decided that my days in sail were over. As I'd finished with the *Saltcote Belle* I had got my customs certificates made out to me, my proof that I had been the Master of a barge trading under sail for a living. In fact I had made quite a good living when freights had been produced for us, but I knew that the barge was not really big enough for Mr Vandersite to get us fixed for outside charters, and that was why we had laid around a lot waiting for orders. It was likely that if we could have lifted a hundred and fifty tons, instead of just one hundred and twenty, we might have stood a much better chance of getting the work, but that was history.

My thoughts had turned to power and it was with that in mind that I gave Mr Kimber of F. T. Everard a call. You can imagine my surprise when, after I had spoken to him for about five minutes, he said, 'What about your old ship the *Greenhithe*? She wants a mate you know.' I told him I had really been thinking about power, and he said that young Ken Fry had just left her to go into power. He came out with the proposition that he could fix me up to go in any ship as AB, or Second Mate in one of the larger coasters, at any time. But first I would have to join the union and acquire a discharge book. I could take him up on his offer, or go back on the *Greenhithe* and change over later. I'm afraid that without much hesitation I chose to rejoin Bob Roberts on the *Greenhithe*.

It was good to be able to stand on her decks again and to take stock of the old familiar surroundings. I then realised that I had let myself in for a lot more hard work, and plenty of wettings. However, I also knew that I would still learn more from being in sail, and that I hadn't quite finished with it.

That same evening I gave Bob a ring, but Mr Kimber had already told him I was rejoining the *Greenhithe*. When I spoke to him he said, 'You must be a glutton for punishment, but I'll be more than glad to have you back.' He said that he looked forward to seeing me on the Monday morning when he would be going back to Greenhithe, as that was where the old girl was lying.

I already knew she was there and had shipped aboard. When I told Bob I was already on her, he asked if I would be going home for the weekend. 'Yes,' I said 'for I'm now courting strong.' He laughed and said that we'd have to earn more money then. I laughed and said that it was my intention to get my ticket before taking the plunge. My young lady had agreed that we should wait at least until then.

Our cargoes were many and varied and in addition we had a fairly steady trade going to the North for coal. Freights to Yarmouth, Norwich, Colchester and Ipswich were our main runs, from which we were getting a good steady living. But we still had the occasional long lies thrown in at times. It seemed as if a pattern developed - a good run followed by a lie for nearly a couple of weeks, before the order would come for Keadby, light.

Loading flour in London one time after we had a quiet spell, we were hoping for a Friday finish. But the dockers didn't quite make it. Bob was really upset as he wanted us to be at Lowestoft for Saturday night, so that we all had a peaceful Sunday. That was not to be, and it was mid-morning before we were able to clear the ship and get ourselves away down from her.

We then started having a change of luck, as one of our bunkering tankers had been working the dock and we were good for a pull down. We not only had the pull, but also the good treatment from the P.L.A. that went with it. We quickly found ourselves out and clear of the Albert Dock, through into the King George and then straight out into the river.

Going down Jim, the third hand and I had been busy. The boat was up in the davits and lashed in and all the preparations had been made for a rough trip. As we turned out of the bottom of Long Reach so Bob had shouted for a 'Let go!' and as soon as the towrope was recovered on board it was down bowsprit. Setting the one jib on the end, the *Greenhithe* became a live thing and she was off.

As we later crossed the tail of the South Whitaker, so the wind was increasing and Bob reckoned we had a good force six, and at times more. We took a few cloths out of the mainsail and stowed the mizzen. She was then a bit lighter on the helm but still the wind increased, until we reckoned we had the gale that was promised to us. By then we were down to topsail sheet, and even with only that Bob said that the way we were going we had plenty of time to get down and into Lowestoft. Our wind was from the south-east and Bob and I were kept busy at the wheel with both of us steering. Jim kept the tea coming. It turned out to be a really dirty night, but not for the *Greenhithe*, as she was continually being swept clean as the seas roared around and over her.

As the daylight came in, so Bob thought the wind fell to about a six, but the breaking seas still made it look a lot more than that. We were getting down off Pakefield and Bob's intentions were to run down inside the Barnard Shoal and so get a look and see if she would 'take the piers' as he put it. He had our Jim busy on the lead line, as the depth of water was one of the things that told Bob what he needed to know as to our whereabouts. He was brought up in those waters and I don't think there was much he couldn't make his mind up about in the area.

Bob decided to have the topsail back on as he would need to drive her in. Jim and I had a fair job to get that topsail back up. We only succeeded when Bob had shook her up into the wind, whilst we hove like a couple of good'uns. Next we had to trim the mainsail and heave down on the vang. Once Bob was satisfied that all was ready, he had me on the wheel with him and Jim was on standby.

As we approached the pier heads I couldn't think what might happen to us. The seas were breaking badly over the south pier head, but we were committed and we couldn't have turned back out if we had wanted to. The instant that we were in, it was down topsail and sheet then, whilst I dropped the bowsprit jib down, got the bobstay up and the anchor off the bow, our Jim had worked like a madman on the brail winch and the mainsail had climbed up to the sprit. Bob then gave the order to down boat and swing in the davits. Somebody had shouted that the bridge was open, so we could go straight through. That, I think, probably saved the day for us. The couple of cloths of mainsail and the foresail were stowed as soon as we had the boat in the water and still we were going hell for leather up the harbour.

As we approached the berth, I could see a few of the Scottish fisherman standing on their boats at our wharf, having just come back from their Sunday morning service. When Bob gave the order to let go, I paid the anchor chain away, but no, the old girl had decided that she wasn't going to swing and come back head to wind. Her stern set in toward the fishing boats and before she had gone far enough around we clouted the outside craft with an almighty wallop. We heard a couple of planks go. The fishermen threw their Bibles down and Bob was told in no uncertain terms what they thought of him. But for all the notice he took of them, they might just as well have said nothing. There was a huge notice telling them that it was a private wharf. At the end of the argument they had to shift so that we could drop in. First we got our stern lines ashore and then we had a long heave up, for she had run about fifteen fathoms of chain out when we had let go the anchor.

Meantime Bob had gone below, and before we were alongside he came on deck again ready for home. He gave Jim and me a good sub and he was off. After we had sorted ourselves out we decided that it was time for a cup of tea, and then turn in for a couple of hours. When we got up we gave the old girl a good harbour stow and made preparations for the discharge of our cargo.

Seeing the bowsprit being hauled up caused quite a stir ashore as it was usually done at sea. The people on the quay paid us many compliments. That evening we were treated to a few pints once the locals knew that we were the lads from the barge that had held up the town, for it appeared the bridge master had swung the bridge without doing half the things that should have been done for the public's safety. I was told that his old grandfather had been a sailing smacksman, so he no doubt knew what a job it is to stop a sailing craft.

After spending a nice couple of days at Lowestoft in good settled weather, Jim and I soon forgot anything of bad or rough trips – the nightlife and good beer saw to that. I'd been along to the agent's office to see if Bob had rung through. He said that we had orders for Keadby light for coal, but the destination port was not known.

We were well used to getting those sort of orders, so when we were writing to our girlfriends we just used to put the one word on the back of the envelope, the return port. The girl who it was for knew the address to write to from that. It was always nice to know that we had orders, as Jim and I could always have a good sub on it and know that we wouldn't be short of fags. Of course, grubstakes were always the top priority and we made sure that we never went short of food.

Our towrope was ready when the tug arrived alongside, but we still hadn't seen Bob. After about half an hour he arrived as puffed out as could be. We were already singled up and soon slipped and away. Shortly after passing outward through the bridge, where a couple of days before we had literally flown through, the wind was still about the same, south-south-east, but without the bite in it. While we had been waiting for Bob to arrive we had got the topsail sheet out, the boat in the davits, plus all the other things that had to be done to get a barge ready for sea.

The old tug pulled us about a mile offshore and we had the lot set when he cast us off. Once the towrope was back on board it was down bowsprit and set the jib. Our jib was always stowed on the bowsprit, not set flying like a lot of the short sea runners. Their jib always seemed to be down the fo'c'sle, and the bowsprit stuck up in the air. The way we used to get a third hand to work on the bowsprit was to let them go out when the barge was empty. They went to the end along the weather side footrope, letting go the jib gaskets as they made their way back on board. As soon as they got back, it was let go the downhaul, swing away on the halyards, and haul the sheets until the jib was set to perfection. I think our Jim used to like me to cheer him on and to hasten him up so we could get a brew going.

I told Bob to get a watch below. We used to really enjoy the watch when we had a nice breeze on our beam, and at those times Bob used to get many a long watch below. When Bob was on the wheel, at the change of watch Jim would go away for'ard to take over from me, and I would go down in the cabin on the locker with a blanket over me, ready for the call. Sleep was never a problem coming, as the hard physical work and all the fresh air made us well tired.

Our passage North went like a dream, and the wind even let us sail up the Humber right to our loading berth at Keadby on the Trent. The wind coming across the Wash had freshened enough to make us drop the topsail, but that was the *Greenhithe's* weather, and when the old girl was like that everyone was more than happy. Quick loading at Keadby meant that we were soon ready to leave, but the way the wind was, and as there wasn't another ship or barge due up, Bob decided that we would have a night's stay. We had another great evening in the Friendship with Bob entertaining on the squeeze box, and then we were back aboard to a good night's sleep below.

A nice moderate westerly greeted us next morning and Bob couldn't get away soon enough, but we had to wait for the tug. It was with us as soon as there was water up to the barge, and as we were singled up ready we passed the towrope, let go the slips, and away we went. Casting off the tow in Hull Roads, Bob kept us on our toes and said that we would have to watch out as the wind was due to increase to a six or seven. As we only had about a four at the time we set the lot. Soon we were leaving the Bull Fort away to starboard and shaping for the Protector buoy.

As we passed out clear of the estuary we still hadn't any noticeable increase in the wind, so Bob decided that he would have a watch below. We slopped away across the Wash, and when we hauled Cromer later, we still hadn't got the blow. However, by the time we were going through the Cockle Gateway, the wind had well freshened, enough to make us down the topsail and reduce the mainsail a few cloths. As we drew into Corton Roads, Bob decided that we might as well bring up for a few hours. Jim was left in charge of the fishing lines and told to keep an eye on her. She lay quietly with the wind just touching off the land, and also head to tide.

The location of this anchorage has been passed down by local seafarers over the years. You knew you were there when the old derelict church is seen open through, you then bring up off the shore to suit the vessel's draft. You can go below and sleep without much fear of dragging, provided you have put sufficient chain out.

Turning out after our few hours rest, we were ready to get on with it again after downing a welcome mug of tea. Then it was heave short the anchor, get the mainsail and mizzen set, and have the foresail ready. It was then set and broke out the anchor for us. We would wind on the windlass furiously to heave up as fast as we could, and then bowse the anchor off. Next we set up the bowsprit and got the jib on. If there was not too much wind, the staysail would be set up over the jib. We then really looked like a sailing ship, from both ashore and aboard.

In a light wind and calm sea the *Greenhithe* shows off her sheer.

The *Greenhithe* was a better ship when she had a coal cargo in, seeming to be a lot more buoyant. Quite different from the dead cargoes of cement or grain. We were all pleased with the way things were going.

After being underway for a couple of hours the wind shifted further round to the north and was freshening all the time. By the time we had rounded Orfordness we had reduced to about two thirds of the mainsail, topsail sheet, foresail, jib and mizzen. Tramping along before a moderate gale the old girl was now in her element, but was once again filled up with water amidships.

When we had passed the Rough Towers and were shaping up the East Swin, we began to get a lee off the shallows of the West Rocks, followed by the Gunfleet Sands, likewise the Buxey and then the Maplin. Once in the area of the Blacktail Spit, Bob had to make a decision whether to stay at the Blacktail or push on in the hope that the wind would moderate and let us take the harbour at Margate, for that was where we were bound.

Bob, being Bob, decided that we would keep going. Running across the shallows we found a heavy broken sea, and it soon became clear to Bob that we were not going to be able to take the harbour when we got down there. Sure enough, once we were down off the Hook, we had no chance to get in the harbour. I consider that this was one of the worst mis-judgements that Bob made whilst I was with him. Not that we were in any trouble, but we ended up having to run down past Margate and then, once we'd got the other side of the North Foreland, Bob tucked us well inside where we dropped anchor.

He was convinced that the wind would last a little time. He was right, of course, and we were to stay there for the next couple of days. We then had to get out with the wind shifted to the east, but at least it had fined away to about a force four. We got back to the correct side of the Foreland, and then Bob had to gill us about to wait for the water to make inside the harbour. As soon as he thought there was water enough he reduced our rig, wanting to hit the sand inside, but not too heavily. We slid round the pier end and we were there at last.

The spell at anchor had done us some good, for the mizzen rigging was quite full of cleaned and gutted fish, and again we were able to live very cheaply. The swell inside the harbour was still there and lying in Margate was never very comfortable once the tide came in. We always surged back and forth. The easterly swell just had to come rolling around the Pier head, and then we were tumbling about as if we were at sea. The time to sleep was once the old girl had sat on the bottom as the tide left us; then we could have a good rest.

After our discharge at Margate had been completed we had to try to get out. We had orders for London light, to load the old grey dust, cement, for Colchester. Jim and I would be well pleased that we were not going to be dragging about the London river awaiting for orders. The wind that had brought us into the harbour now stopped us from getting out. Our course up along the land was about west by north and this fair wind was blowing away.

As there was no tug there, it was left to Bob to try to get a couple of fishermen to get us out clear.

It took a lot of persuading to convince a couple of small fishing boats that they would be able to hold us and get us a couple of hundred yards offshore. A time was set to catch the next day's tide, and as soon as we floated we swung the vessel round to head out, then hove down on to the pier head where the fishing boats were going to pick us up. Once we had got on the pier head, we set the topsail and eased the mainsail out just beyond the sprit. By that time the fishing boats were waiting at our bows and we passed down a line to each. As soon as they had taken the strain we slipped our quay rope and were off. As we cleared the pier head we let the boats go, had the gear set up and made good progress.

It was quite a pleasant sail along the Kentish shore and through the Four Fathom Channel. Coming clear of the shoals we found a very heavy swell running from the north-east, but the wind was still well from the east and we thought how lucky we were. It was at times like that that barging becomes a real pleasure.

When we arrived at Greenhithe, Bob put us alongside the ship's buoy. Two buoys at Greenhithe were put down for Everard ships to lie to. We often used these buoys as the tide ran very hard in the bight and it was no place to lie to anchor.

We were loading our stores the next morning when we got the order to go over to the Tunnel works to load our cement. We were to go to the jetty's inside berth. I found Everards boatman 'Brusher' and he soon had hold of us and lugged us across the river and put us alongside. That berth was very awkward to get into without a tow. We were always told to make use of the motorboat when we could.

During the early evening we made ready for loading, and before midnight we were battened down ready for sea. Sometime after midnight we were called and told it was raining, but by then we were all done. I knew that Bob was unlikely to join us over there, so I had been in touch with 'Brusher' to make sure that he would come over and get us. When the high water had made, Jim and I were just slipping out with the first drain of the ebb tide. We let our head come into the tide and Jim said, 'Here comes the boat.' Bob jumped aboard and I passed over the tow rope and with a quick slip we were free of the jetty and clear.

As soon as we came head to wind we got all the usual gear set. Turning away down river the wind seemed to be increasing, and we were just down below Corytown when an extra heavy one hit us. The topsail was rucked and a few cloths taken out of the mainsail, and the old girl was a lot better for it. We were not so wet in the waist and it was more or less one hand to the wheel.

At times like those we didn't push the old girl too much, for with the wind right ahead we knew that we would be bringing up on the low water anyway, to lie the flood. We would get underway again on the high water slack. As things turned out we were able to get down to just above the Blacktail Spit and there the old girl lay comfortably, head to wind and tide. It was the turn of the fishing lines to go over, and some fish were caught before we had our lie down. When we turned out later four more fish were on our hooks.

Getting underway in conditions like those that day was always a bit of a problem. The old girl would lie back on her chain and it was slow and hard work to heave up. Setting the sails was no problem for the barge was still head to wind, and Bob had the strength of Jim and me together. He always gave us a hand with the heavy work when he could. The foresail, being backed to windward, soon had Bob paying off on the tack he wanted and we set the bowsprit jib. The old girl then became very wet because Bob thought we had a good chance of getting through the Spitway, or at least to stop in it and save the anchor work. He was reluctant to drop the topsail at all, so although we could have done without it, Bob held on and drove her hard.When we arrived at the Spitway we found a very heavy short cross sea. Bob said that as soon as we got a little lee from the Gunfleet Sand, we'd have the leeboards right up and drop the head of the topsail. With the ebb setting us away from the Buxey Sand we were able to find water through which was very smooth, and so were not too concerned about touching. Bob said that we would have lain in there quietly enough had the *Greenhithe* taken the ground.

Once we had passed through the Spitway Bob decided to let her keep going and passed her over to me, with orders to take her up into the Colne and bring up where I liked so that Jim and I could fish. The Colne was not worked after dark above Prior's Wharf at Fingringhoe in those days, and I decided that just inside the Colne, beyond the heavy swell, would do us.

Once the lines were down the fish were not long in coming aboard. Again we were to be surprised. Bob had been busy below and had boiled some of the fish caught earlier, mixed the fish with boiled spuds, and then the potatoes and fish had been fried to a nice crisp golden brown. They were really smashing, washed down with a couple of mugs of tea. After that we had a nice piece of fried duff and treacle with more tea. Once again we set the lines.

Bob gave us a very early call next morning so that we could all have our breakfast before doing any work. However, Jim had checked and rebaited his lines before he came down for his breakfast which was, yes, more fish. That time it was kippers. Bob, unknown to us, had brought them aboard and, rather than take them back home, had cooked them for us to enjoy. They were followed by the old traditional bread and jam. I don't think that kippers go down well in a lot of folks' homes and I never did discover if Mrs. Roberts would have minded.

Jim and I soon had the old girl underway when Bob was happy to leave. On the way we had plenty of time to heave the bowsprit up. The little motor boat was ready for us by the time we had passed Alresford Creek, and before we arrived at Colchester we had a very fine harbour stow with the hatches cleared ready for our discharge. Unfortunately it was not to be that day, so we could take it easy.

Bob was of course away to catch his train for home, there to await the call from the broker to tell him the next freight. I would call him at home once we had cleared the cargo and got *Greenhithe* ready for sea again. Around that time Bob had decided to move from his Bexleyheath home down to a cottage by the green at Pin Mill. The move was all being sorted out by his 'good lady' as he was mostly away in the old barge.

On one occasion, whilst we were having a few jobs done on the yard, Bob came to ask me if I would like to crew for him in his smack whilst he was taking it down to Pin Mill. I jumped at the offer as I had never before been aboard a sailing smack. His craft, the *Stormy Petrel*, was kept at the Erith Yacht Club which was only just up the road from Greenhithe, so it was easy to get there and spend a day with Bob checking her gear out. As a busy barge master Bob had only a limited amount of time available to spend on the upkeep of his smack. In

the event, we found that there was very little that had to be done. We did load some bits and pieces from his household, only the likes of a bit of linoleum and a few odds and ends from his shed made up our 'cargo', but there was enough to give us a good old clutter around her decks. When we had done all our preparations Bob said that the forecast was for a south-easterly breeze, so we would leave our departure until the following day.

When I arrived at Erith next morning it was about ten o'clock and our planned sailing time was supposed to be around

The fishing smack *Stormy Petrel* did a removal job when Bob Roberts moved house from Bexleyheath to Pin Mill.

ten thirty. But by the time Bob had had a natter, first with one chum, then another, it got to be nearer midday before we left. However, once we were on board it took but a few moments to get the sails set. Casting adrift the buoy, Bob brought us around and onto the starboard tack and we set off with our fresh south-easterly. To me it felt great to stand aboard her and feel the difference in the way she heeled compared to the old *Greenhithe's* jerking sprawl. With the ebb running beneath her, '*Stormy*' was really going and Bob kept up the pace. The cold was the worst thing.

As we neared the Spitway the wind had gone further to the east and Bob reckoned that we were in for a blow. He decided that we would keep going down outside the Gunfleet sand to make sure that we would make use of all our tide. The swells were by that time running long and heavy, but still we took no water on board. Eventually I could look away to port and see the north-east Gunfleet buoy; then I knew that we would soon come about again on the starboard tack and shape up for the Medusa.

On that point of sailing we had a bit of slack in the sheets and we were soon making rapid progress. As we passed the Medusa and then the Stone Banks buoy all the sightings for the harbour at Harwich unfolded before us. With this fair and very strong wind the *Stormy Petrel* soon made her way up to Collimer Point and a smart gybe got us on the tack for the Pin Mill moorings. Soon after passing the point Bob had me stow up the jib and get the anchor ready. Once he was ready it was down helm and '*Stormy*' roared round into the wind with the shout, 'Let go the anchor!' After stowing the mainsail I said to Bob that I had not seen any water come aboard. He just laughed and said, 'Of course. You obviously haven't sailed in a smack before.'

On gaining the shore after we had cleared up, Bob was able to confirm which mooring had been laid for him. We took the lino and other odds and ends up to his new home and enjoyed tea and cake as our reward!

Chapter XVII
SMOKE LESS FAGS

By that time work was again starting to tail off, and what there was went into the motor barges. My thoughts once again turned to the question of going into power. Somehow it was a very difficult choice to have to make. I liked the sailing craft better, but the money was by then very bad and at that time there were more and more barges being laid up. We were more fortunate than most as we could always go back to Keadby to load coal. All the time that we lay about Bob would sail with his grub bag on his back between home and the barge. After we had lain for nearly a couple of weeks, he said, 'Tomorrow, if we've no orders, we'll go to Keadby for coal.'

We were starting to roll the old fag ends again so we were really looking forward to having a good sub. I thought to myself what the hell am I doing out here for nothing. It was the beginning of the end for me in that berth, much as I enjoyed my time with Bob.

He came aboard the next morning with more spring in his step. The first thing he said was to pick up the bowsprit, as we had orders to go to the inside berth at Johnson's to load cement for Colchester. Everything went right for us that time; we had a nice quick load, a brilliant sail down to the Colne, and a short tow up to Colchester. All went as smoothly as could be and we were soon empty.

After sweeping the hold out we received our orders for Keadby light, to load more coal for the Harwich gas works. We could be sure of a few bob for a while, as at any time that we had orders for anything, Bob was as keen as mustard to get on with the job. Once we had the orders, the wind was doing its best to stop us making our passage. We lay at Colchester for a couple of days whilst it blew very strongly from the north-east. On the third day, Bob jumped aboard and said, 'We're off.' As soon as the motor boat came up to the quay for us, we were ready to slip, and so with little effort the line was passed, we let go and were away.

Our motor boat had hailed to say that, as he wasn't that busy, he would keep hold of us until we got down to Freshwater Jetty. That would be a better start for us. By the time we were passing Wivenhoe shipyard we had most of the sail on the old girl. As soon as we let go the tug I hove the bobstay down and then was able to set up the topsail, followed by the bowsprit jib. Then the *Greenhithe* was really away with a bone in her teeth. Bob had told me shortly after leaving that the best we could hope for would be to get ourselves into Harwich, although there might be more problems in getting ourselves ashore. We had a grand sail down the Wallet with plenty of slamming, for with the tide running down to the north-east and the wind being about force six from the east, there was quite some swell with a breaking sea. It wasn't until we had rounded the Naze that we got any relief. Once we could steer north for the harbour the weather then came onto our beam and we soon ate up the few remaining miles to allow us to anchor just off Shotley pier. Bob was soon ashore without a problem to catch his bus home to Pin Mill. As Bob left us he said he wouldn't be back unless we got a change of wind direction to suit.

Next day there was no sign of any change so Jim and I rigged out the barge boat ready for a sail. As soon as that was done we were off, and with our beam wind, were soon tying up at Halfpenny Pier at Harwich. We made our way slowly up to The Flag pub where I was able to contact the union boss I'd come to see. By leaving the price of a few pints of beer behind the bar and promising him I would pay my subs regularly I was given my card, and that's how I got into the seaman's union. The next item I needed, a discharge book, was nearly as easy. The union chap said he could get me fixed up in a berth without the book, but I don't think I would have got the rating that I was entitled to.

After lying a couple of days the weather had started to fine down and Bob decided to have a go. But after sailing the full ebb down, the sea became much too much for the old *Greenhithe*. Bob said that if we anchored until the next high water we still wouldn't get anywhere, and maybe wouldn't get our anchor in, so we ended up with a run back to the anchorage which we had left just a few hours before. Bob was away off home again. 'I'll see you when the weather changes.' he said again, and with a few of our hard won fish in his bag for his family's supper, he was on his way. I told Bob that I would be going to Parkstone Quay the next day if we were not sailing. He said that I should wait until an hour before high water and if he hadn't showed up that would mean that we were not going to sea.

Next day came and still no change appeared in the weather, and as Bob hadn't appeared by a good hour before the high water I was off with the old boat. Although it was no yacht it would soon blow up the river, and when I wanted to come away the tide would be with me for tacking back down. Jim decided that he would stay aboard as it was so bitterly cold.

I had to take the chance to get myself and my future sorted out. After I told the Parkstone people of my history, and showed them some of my discharges, they did a little research of their own and decided that I was eligible for my AB's rating under the Merchant Shipping Act 1906, paragraph 58. And so I became an able-bodied seaman. I had my papers and I could seek employment in power craft, deep sea or coastwise whenever it might suit me.

Tacking back down the river with my new found qualification had me thinking about switching to power again. But once I was down towards the old *Greenhithe*, I knew from just looking at her that it was going to take more than just a lean period to get me out of her.

Jim was asleep when I got back on board, but he had had quite a bit of luck fishing. Even as I pulled in the lines he had left out we had a couple more fish. We used to catch what we could whilst at anchor, as most of the pubs that we went to would see us all right for a couple of beers in exchange for a few fish. Bait came free to us, all we had to do was to dig anywhere we were and stick it on the hook; in those times we could nearly always catch fish wherever we were.

About six o'clock one evening we got a loud hail from the shore and there stood Bob. I had guessed that we might hear from him as the wind had gone into the south and fined to about a force four. On boarding he said, 'I think we'll have another go,' and soon Jim and I had the windlass handles shipped and were getting on with the job of heaving short. Bob was below getting into some heavy weather gear, for the night was going to be a long and cold one. Once we were underway it became a routine trip for us.

Bob was usually in high spirits when the *Greenhithe* had the wind on her quarter as she had then, but he said that it was going to blow before the night was out. By the time we were off Lowestoft the wind was backing to the south-east and blowing a lot harder than when we left. Still, as long as it didn't easter any more the old girl would continue to blow along nicely on a reduced rig and seemed to glory in the conditions.

Soon, it seemed, we were passing through Hull Roads and Bob said that he was going to tuck us into the back of the Whiting Sands for a few hours. We would be sailing up to Keadby on the next tide. None of us got much sleep as we roared about at anchor, and I'm sure that we were all glad when it was time to get away again and before long we had arrived at Keadby.

Everard's *Cambria* and another mulie beyond at Keadby, both loaded and waiting for the tug.

By sailing the barge head up onto the shore the tide soon had us swung around to drop straight into the loading berth. We were loaded straight away as there were no other craft up on our tide. We decided to lie until the next day, as it was blowing quite hard from the south-east, and that meant that we had another very enjoyable evening in the Friendship.

The dawn was very grey and overcast, with a very strong wind from the south-east, and it was raining as well for good measure. But the tug had been ordered and was with us in very good time, for they knew the importance of the next ebb to us and they also liked to get past the junction where the Trent and the Ouse split before the ebb came away too hard. It was a nasty bend there and the old *Greenhithe*, like most barges, didn't steer too well behind a powerful tug. Our run down to Hull Roads went well and gave us the chance to make doubly sure that everything was for the very rough trip that I was sure we were in for.

Setting sail was no problem, for Bob had decided to keep the topsail stowed. We just set the mainsail, the mizzen, and had the foresail ready. As the tug pulled us clear of the craft anchored in Hull Roads, he let out a resounding cock-a-doodle-doo on his whistle, and then cast us adrift. The third hand and I whipped the towrope in as fast as we were able and, without a shout from aft, set the foresail up and got the towrope lashed away before lowering the bowsprit and getting the jib on her. In that rig the *Greenhithe*, with the tide, could just about tackle anything that the elements could throw at her, provided that we were about to handle things. But we all knew that we could easily be overcome if we got it wrong. A good Skipper had to make decisions that would ensure a safe ship at the same time as being a profitable one. With those things in Bob's mind he told me that we would be anchoring in the Spurn Gat, and he just hoped that the wind didn't back and trap us.

As we drew further down the river the seas were getting bigger and I could see why Bob had decided to stop. Getting into the gat caused us no problems, for Bob just arrived at the entrance, bore away, and we were sort of in. Then the orders came fast. It was stow the mizzen as we shaped in, and then down the jib and up with the bobstay. Next, as I stood by the anchor, Jim was ready to drop the foresail. On the shout from Bob the

Bob Roberts, standing second from the right amongst the racing crew aboard Everard's *Dreadnought* which he had just skippered in the 1963 Centenary Thames Barge Match which, at the time, was expected to be the last. The reverse of this photograph is poignantly captioned 'Towing home for the last time.' The *Dreadnought* was broken up less than a year later.

foresail was dropped and as he spun the wheel to shoot us up into the wind there came the call, 'Let go!' and I gave her thirty fathoms on the windlass. Bob came forward to give the chain a touch, just to make sure that we were not dragging. With the way that we had sailed the anchor in I was convinced there was no fear of that happening.

If a barge's anchor is sailed home with the craft having its full weight behind it, in the *Greenhithe* about two hundred and fifty tons, there was usually no need to worry. Once the barge has 'rode' to its chain you also have little fear of a fouled anchor.

After our evening meal Bob said that with the way it was blowing we would be having the night in there, hoping that the wind didn't veer to trap us on a lee shore whilst in the creek. Luck was with us overnight for the wind next morning was still from the east-south-east, but had decreased to about a force four. Bob had us out early to get a good breakfast and, well fed, about a couple of hours before the flood had finished funnelling into the Humber we were moving out close hauled on the port tack. As we came clear of the creek the old girl had all the gear set plus the bowsprit jib, and we were off in fine form. She was certainly throwing the water about as we shook the swells apart, so we were sure of a good wetting whenever we had the need to go forward.

Bob decided to have the first watch below and I think that was because he had spent the greater part of the night looking out of the cabin hatch to make sure all was well whilst Jim and I slept. He needed a couple of hours to top up his sleep. Bob said on going below, 'Give me a call in three hours unless you need me before, and keep standing off on a tight sheet unless anything major happens.'

I knew that if I gave a good boot kick on the deck Bob would have been up like a rabbit out of the cabin hatchway, but I had a very good watch and Bob appeared without a call at the end of his three hours, which to us was like a good night's sleep when under way. We had a good brew up and then Bob sent me below. After a couple of hours down Bob caught a very heavy squall, and it was my turn to jump when his boot stamping had me up on deck and flying along to drop the head of the topsail, and then get a couple of cloths out of the mainsail. Soon we had her all snugged down again without getting too wet. If the *Greenhithe* had been on the other tack the halyard and brail winch would have been under water and I would have been very wet.

Returning aft it was, 'Put the kettle on, mate.' Our Jim was out of the way below because he hadn't been too well for a couple of days. Not seasick, I might say. I think it was too much beer. But he was okay next day, back to his usual chirpy self. After we had settled the old girl, Bob went off watch with a 'Call me if you want me,' and I was left to my own thoughts and dreams again.

I think that the times when one was alone were the best times to teach yourself something new. It was always the same with me, to have something written down and in my pocket. The many hours that I spent on my own were the times when I taught myself the rules and regulations of the sea, which I could soon repeat, parrot fashion. Likewise the formulae that applied to navigation were mostly learnt on a windswept barge's deck. I guess that more than once Jim must have thought that I was talking to myself. All you sailing students out there might like to try it, for there is too much going on everywhere else to allow these things to be properly learned otherwise.

Bob had enjoyed a few more well deserved hours below when I think he had noticed that we were sailing along at a much lesser angle of heel. Whilst he had been below the wind had blown itself around well to the north of west and was a nice steady force four. I got Jim up to hold the wheel whilst I gave her the full mainsail and hove up the topsail. We were certainly slipping through the water with a lot less effort, and getting along well. When Bob saw things for himself he said, 'I think we'll have the wind out from the north-west before long.' After a good mug, I was soon away for my watch below.

Called from my watch below without a boot thumping on the deck was nice. I poked my head up to Bob's usual words, 'Put the kettle on, mate,' and soon Bob and I were having a few moments together that only a pair who can get along, and have the old craft at heart, could share. After about half an hour it was time for me to get below again, for with a barge on a coastal passage you didn't know when you'd be called out, or for what reason. Whilst we could, we slept and ate as long as we were able, and when having an easy sail, as we were then, a barging life couldn't be bettered.

Bob had always said to me that the barge would be finished in my time, and I should prepare myself for a life in ships if I intended to spend my days afloat. He was right, for our own company was getting a great fleet of coasters and was in fierce competition with the Dutch who were undercutting all the prices. The sailing barge had no way of knowing where the next freight was for, or even if there was going to be another one. But our old firm had a very soft spot for barges, at least whilst Mr Fred and Mr Will Everard were alive.

As we followed our passage along the coast my mind turned to the future and was made up. We were doing a lot more of the Humber runs, and I knew that the money was good, but not when we were going back light so many times. I decided I would give notice to Bob, once we got to Harwich, that I would leave next time that we went onto the yard again. We knew that we were getting close to being called to the yard for our annual survey, so that was to be when I would go.

On the change of the watch, and as we were having our usual yarn, I told Bob what I had decided to do. He said that he wouldn't try and stop me for I was doing the right thing. He also knew that I had to go soon to log the time on ship's articles. This would allow me to get paid when I went to college to try for my ticket. I wanted to go for it as soon as I was twenty or twenty-one, but that's another story.

Off Felixstowe, near the old Cork Light Vessel, we made our high water, and with the wind by then out of the north, Bob knew that we would have to go to anchor outside the harbour. Just as we got up to the Platters, Bob shot us in as close as he dared, and there we let go. The riding light was hoisted and then we then went down below to await the next low water.

After our five-hour lie it was up again and a nice mug inside us, heave short, and get all the working sails set before breaking the anchor out. We made short work of the sail up to the harbour. We had to make a few boards before we were able to get to windward of the Guard buoy and could fetch up along the Harwich shore. Once off the train ferry jetty Bob rounded us up so we could get the mainsail and mizzen off her. And then, as he bore away for the creek we stowed the foresail and then got the head of the topsail out of the way. Bob drove her through the dark for the last few yards so the old *Greenhithe* came to a stop in the soft mud of the creek, ready for discharge. Jim and I uncovered the hatches before we turned in for the last part of the night, as those Harwich folk have a habit of starting very early in the morning, and we didn't want their early callout. After lying in until about nine in the morning, Bob came for'ard, pushed the kettle over the stove and said, 'What about breakfast then?'

Bob was able to get home fairly easily from there. The Navy ran their own trot boat across to Shotley from Harwich at the time, enabling Bob to catch his bus home from there. Bob appeared a couple of days after we had discharged with more and better news for us.

162 We had lain in the gas works' creek for two days hearing nothing, and Jim and I were fed up. Thinking that Bob would jump aboard at any time we hadn't roamed far away from the *Greenhithe*, at least whilst there was water enough for us to get out of the creek. We knew that once Bob came aboard he would be ready to go. I think we had had enough of roaming about Harwich and, knowing it was to be my last trip, I was looking forward to going to Greenhithe, and my paying off.

True to form Bob jumped aboard just as we were coming afloat. He soon checked our situation and at the same time asked me if the hold was ready. As mate it was my job to have completed the clean up, which I told him I had. Bob said, 'Good, as we have been blessed with a cargo of straw from Colchester to Ridham Dock in Kent for the paper mills.' I was very pleased, because it meant that I would have a

few quid to settle up with. Straw cargo was worth £1.6s.6d. (£1.33) a ton to the barge at the time and the old *Greenhithe* picked up about forty tons. The freight money was divided 50% to our firm and 50% to the barge. The Skipper's share was 66% of the barge's, and my share would be the remainder. These were less half of the crew's expenses, tugs, dues, etc. and also half the third hand's wages. It can be seen that we didn't get very rich.

We were soon sorted, the boat up in the davits, and even the bowsprit went down before we left. We had a

Greenhithe under full sail and on the wind.

good strong wind about south, so we were in for a right thrashing to windward. As soon as we had slacked the mainsail out to the sprit and set the foresail aback, the *Greenhithe* was ready so we let go the mooring warps and were off.

After leaving the berth Bob had us setting all the working canvas that the *Greenhithe* could carry, except the mizzen. As the tide would be against us for quite a few miles Bob was determined to push as hard as we could. Getting out of the harbour certainly took it out of us, laying on our beam ends. The short tacks were not what the *Greenhithe* liked. Once clear of the harbour Bob was able to push us away offshore and make better use of the tide, and soon we were clawing our way around

Walton on the Naze. When the tide did ebb we were able to use it on our lee bow and so the few miles up the Wallet were done in great style. As we passed the Knoll buoy the wind had backed to about south by south-east and reached about force six, perhaps seven at times. Bob had us stow up the jib and take up the bowsprit and drop the head of the topsail. Still we were bowling along well over the ebb tide that was pushing outwards from the River Colne. Bob said, 'We'll go till we stop.' That was up into Marriages Bight, just past Alresford Creek, when we suddenly slid to a halt from about four knots. We stowed up and turned in for a well-earned rest.

Long before the birds had started their dawn chorus the *Greenhithe* had started to lift to the tide, and that was the signal for us to be on our way. As the wind was still blowing hard from the south it was a fair wind up the river. Quickly the topsail and staysail were set to catch the best of the wind from over the fields, trees and buildings as we slowly made our way up stream.

When we arrived at the head of the river we found our loading berth empty. After we slipped our head rope ashore we were able to swing our craft, and lie head down the river ready to load, and also ready to slip away once we had received our straw. The cargo for us did not start to arrive until about midday, so we knew that we would get at least one night in port, and a few pints would be enjoyed in the Anchor that evening. All through the next day cargo kept arriving, but we had so much rain that nobody wanted to work, and we didn't finish until well into our third day. It was then down to us to prepare the *Greenhithe* for sea.

Lots of lashing down had to be done with wires and tackles to try and keep the huge stack in place. All the temporary works like moving the main and fore sheets over the stack top were completed using heavy wires. The stowing system of the mainsail had to be sorted out, including altering the main brails, lowers, middles and the peaks; lots of extra work for so little reward.

Two more days were to pass before we could think about leaving as it was still blowing very hard, and thick with rain. We lay not far from the pub and shops and we were more than content. Before we left a little bit of luck came our way. One of our company's motor ships arrived from the North with a cargo of coal. The Master and Bob were good friends and it was agreed that we would pass over our sea towing gear, and we would all leave the quay together. He would then tow us up to Sheerness. He would still have plenty of time to berth in the London River on the next high water.

Leaving the quayside, the hardest part of the trip started for us, and that was to try and steer the *Greenhithe* down river behind the ship. Our stack was so great we couldn't see the ship from the wheel. After passing through Marriage's Bight and clearing Alresford Creek and Freshwater loading jetty, Bob said, 'Lock the steering and slack the towrope out.' From then on the old girl steered herself and, as Bob said, 'If it doesn't get any worse she'll be alright.' She reared and sheered about all the way up the Swin channel until we were able to bring up just below Sheerness along the Cant Edge.

Our tow rope was retrieved as the ship let it go, and with a toot on the whistle he set off heading for the Swatchway channel that links the River Medway to the River Thames. Having our tow up was not to be much to our advantage as we had to lie windbound for the next couple of days. It blew a living gale from out of the south, and with our stack all we could do was to hope things held on. We caught up with sleeping and reading, and of course our windbound occupation of fishing. After catching our first fish we always used to chop it up for use as fresh bait.

We turned out for breakfast on the third day and Bob was well browned off by the high wind. I am not sure that there was any less of it, but he said that we would be off after we had had our breakfast. We had time to get squared away below decks, and then the struggle began for us to heave up the anchor and get the old girl underway. And what a struggle that was. We were lying straight back from our anchor, and with a barge like the *Greenhithe* blowing back with the big straw stack it was a good three-man job to recover our ground tackle. Finally Bob said, 'Right, lads, that's it, let's get some sail on her.' He had to have all the topsail, plus about half the mainsail and the foresail so as to have some sort of control over the old girl.

Once we were underway Bob had hold of her until we at last rounded Garrison Point and were inside Sheerness. He then went to the top of the straw stack whilst I struggled to follow his steering directions, with Jim giving a helping hand as needed. We arrived at Ridham Dock without mishap, but we did have some hairy moments on the way.

As soon as we arrived alongside, the foreman gave us a shout and said that as they had a ship due for the berth where we were, would we move some way ahead. He forecast a wait of up to three days before we could be unloaded, but if we could get the lashings off quickly he could get us out in the next few hours. That was too good to miss and the lashings went flying so that we could take him up on his offer and get discharged there and then. Our cargo went out in just under three hours, the lashings were thrown into the hold together with anything else that we didn't need on our trip round to Greenhithe, and the beams and hatch boards were soon in place. Bob said not to worry about the hatch cloths as the old girl was going to be sorted out when we got on the shipyard.

We let go our ropes and, after we had got a line across to the south side of the dock, we hauled across to get to windward before we set any sail. This was made all the more hair-raising by the wind still blowing like hell from the south and the evening being very dark. Bob had phoned the bridge so we would get a lift without any problem. The topsail was fully set, the mainsail about two thirds set and the foresail backed to starboard to shove our head away to the east. The old girl must have known she was going home for she was on her best behaviour and did everything that Bob asked of her that night. What a real treat it was to be going down through the grounds, and the way we were shifting it wasn't long before the lights of Sheerness were showing over the starboard bow. Once we were past the Naval craft and their unlit buoys we went out past the jetty at Garrison Point, and ran on through the Swatchway for the Thames.

We were able to hold a course up Sea Reach which took us into the Lower Hope. As we closed the weather shore Bob's order came to stow the mainsail. We rounded up into the wind and downed the foresail before letting go the anchor. The topsail was dropped as soon as we were steady head to wind, but the topsail sheet was left out ready for the next tide's muster.

Next morning's mug of tea for Jim and me was to be a little sad. My next move was to be into power craft, and poor old Jim had received his call-up papers to be a soldier. We both knew that when Bob gave us the shout to heave short and get 'em set, that it would be for the last time.

It was still blowing very hard and the rain was lashing down. Bob wasn't very cheerful when he came forward for his cup of tea. We both thought it was something to do with us both leaving, but Bob didn't let on if it was. Our trip up the river to Greenhithe went quite well but was tinged with sadness. When we were nearly ready to stow the sails, old 'Brusher' and his motor boat appeared and rounded up alongside. Jim and I could now give the old girl our final harbour stow, whilst he headed us for our yard berth, where we and the yard hands soon had the *Greenhithe* snugly moored.

Our last evening together was spent in the White Hart and quite a bit of booze was supped. Bob even managed a few tunes on the old squeeze box. It was a very sad next day when Jim and I collected our stamps and money, Jim destined for the army and me to go as able seaman in a cross channel ferry.

A good few years were to pass before my next encounter with the *Greenhithe*, and it was very hard to take in. It was when I was Mate of the Motor Vessel *Security*, one of the larger cargo vessels of

Everard's *Security* was typical of the larger units of the fleet, at a time when sailing barges, though few, still traded under the Everard flag.

the Everard fleet. We had gone to load a cargo over at the Tunnel cement works and there we found the poor old *Greenhithe*, stripped of all her gear, rusting and unkempt, in a black oozing mud berth, used as a lighterman's rest.

Many more years were to be spent by me tramping the globe, but I was able to do that in some comfort and get a reasonable wage for doing it. My experience under sail stood me in great stead, and for all my future employers I was able to give top service, a result of the sometimes harsh, but always beneficial, schooling of the Thames sailing barges.

166   This true story took place more than half a century ago. It reveals many aspects of a certain way of life alien in today's world. Conditions were tough. A wage dependent on the weather and other criteria far beyond the influence, let alone control of the skipper and crew, meant uncertainty was on the daily menu during the final days of coastal sail. Nowadays a formal qualification would be the prerequisite of command, a status unachievable when Ivan became Master of the sailing barge *Saltcote Belle* at such a young age.

    Ivan left the *Greenhithe* during July 1949 and shipped aboard the old train ferry steamship *Essex Ferry* as an Able Seaman. Just before the Christmas he took a similar job aboard the *Thomas M*, built in Holland in 1938, a motor coaster of 507 Gross Tons owned by Metcalf Motor Coasters of London. He stayed in her for seven months before joining the new 1490 Gross Tons *Security*, a handsome coaster completed in June 1950 by the Goole Shipbuilding & Repair Company for F. T. Everard and Sons of Greenhithe. They owned a considerable fleet of steam and motor coasters, sailing barges, tugs and lighters, a shipyard and sail loft. Ivan was promoted to 2nd Mate by the October and 1st Mate nine months later. It was the type of ship where officers dressed in their smart uniforms for dinner.

    His next ship was more down-to-earth; the same company's 'Chant' *Fixity*, one of a class of smaller, austere wartime-built prefabricated coasting vessels, also built at Goole, as the *Empire Fairhaven* in 1944. She was of 410 Gross Tons and had been purchased by Everards during 1946. Ivan's aspirations for advancement were met upon being promoted Master of the *Fixity* within the month.

    His next move was a temporary transfer to the older *Apricity*, a coaster built at Greenock in 1933, where he served as 1st Mate again until taking command of the slightly smaller and even older *Assiduity*, also Greenock built. Following just a week in the tanker *Austility*, built at Sunderland in 1946 as the *Forreria*, Ivan moved into new tonnage as 1st Mate of the Goole built *Singularity* of 1566 Gross Tons for six weeks during 1952. He then took on the same role in the *Speciality* for six months, before returning to the *Singularity* in which he remained until leaving Everards in May 1954.

    Ivan then returned to the traditional Thames Estuary and coastwise trade. He joined the small motor vessel *Success*, a former coasting sailing barge built of steel in Holland as the *Cymric* for London owners in 1903. The *Success* was owned by The London & Rochester Trading Company of Strood in Kent, a similar operation to Everards, but known to the coasting fraternity as the 'Forty Thieves'!

Amidst the winter snow at Ipswich, Ivan tackles a job aboard R. & W. Paul's *Thalatta*.

In 1958 Ivan stepped back in time and went mate on the wooden spritsail barge *Thalatta* which was, of course, the first he had sailed on when in his early teens. 'Young Bob' Wells was Skipper and she also carried a boy third hand, Stanley Missen. Owned by R. & W. Paul, the barge was mainly employed in her owner's London to Ipswich trade, with an occasional cargo to their wharf at Faversham.

The *Thalatta* had been 'modernised' with the installation of an auxiliary engine in 1949 which shared part of the after hold and part of the traditional Master's cabin. The mainsail, topsail and foresail remained and a wheelhouse had been added. During the time Ivan was aboard it was decided to remove her worn out sailing gear and leeboards, relying entirely on the engine, leaving the foresail and a new try-sail as steadying sails. Her redundant steel sprit later replaced the condemned wooden spar on the same owner's sailing barge *Marjorie*.

During 1958 'Government Contractors' H. R. Mitchell & Sons based at the Royal Arsenal, South Woolwich, purchased two ex. Government motor vessels and later a much larger third that had been running supplies to the forts in the Thames Estuary.

Ivan initially went Skipper of the smaller *Vawdrey*, built in Plymouth in 1928, of 93 Gross Tons, but later took the 1929 Faversham built *Geoffrey Stanley* of 98 Gross Tons. Both vessels were used for transporting ammunition, but could occasionally be seen at such barge ports as Maldon with wheat, or Fingringhoe with maize.

The *Katharine Mitchell* was the third vessel, of 177 Gross Tons built at Leith in 1930. Superfluous accommodation aft of the bridge was removed and a cargo

The *Katharine Mitchell*, with the much smaller *Geoffrey Stanley* beyond

hold built, but sceptics wondered how viable the expensive conversion would be. She looked similar to a steamship with her counter stern and raised fo'c'sle head. All three vessels had yellow painted Widdop engines, the *Katharine Mitchell* having two, being twin screw.

Ivan became Master of their *Katharine Mitchell*, often engaged in the carriage of ammunition from Felixstowe Dock to Zeebrugge in Belgium. He once delivered a general cargo into Faversham Dock which must have been a tight squeeze through the bridge and lock gates for such a large vessel.

At the end of 1960 Ivan again returned to barge work, becoming Skipper of the steel motor barge *Adieu*, his wife Pam as mate. The barge was owned by M. F. Horlock (Dredging) Co. Ltd. of Mistley in Essex, one of many vessels employed in the busy sand and ballast trade to Sittingbourne with materials to construct the M2 Motorway. The *Adieu* was built as a sailing barge for Frederick W. Horlock at Mistley in 1929, one of the last of her kind. She and the similar *Reminder* were both unrigged and motorised in 1949. At the same time the mast deck was removed, replaced with a long single hatchway for carrying dragline excavator machinery from Ipswich to ships in the docks near London for export. By the time Ivan and Pam shipped aboard the *Adieu* little trace remained of her sailing origins. She seemed dogged by poor machinery, her various engines seemingly below par for reliability.

Ivan splicing rigging wire for Horlock's *Remercie*.

On Christmas Eve 1963, the James & Stone shipyard at Brightlingsea completed a huge refit, including a 'new' Gleniffer engine removed from an overworked London dock tosher, new steering gear and new wheelhouse combined with new deck accommodation. The shipyard engineers tried for three days to start her engine, but failed. Engineers from the manufacturers managed to bring it to life after the Christmas Holiday. Before the Hazeltons left the *Adieu* in October 1966, she had been re-engined once more, with a Perkins diesel installed, which again had been less than satisfactory in operation. When they came ashore Ivan went into the construction industry, working for Faircloughs until his retirement.

What of the other craft he served aboard or which get a mention? The fate of a few may be unclear, others are recorded and a surprising number survive.

The *Greenhithe* was one that didn't have the long life associated with many iron and steel sailing barges. Everards purchased her 'at the right price' in 1923 when on the stocks at Fellowes Shipyard, Gt. Yarmouth, a newly built but unaccepted steel hull. She never had an engine and finished up unrigged, moored head-in alongside a jetty below Purfleet, her cabin used as a lightermen's and night watchmen's mess room. Eventually the rusting and cement dust covered *Greenhithe* was towed away to Grays and scrapped when just over 30 years old.

Everard's *Will Everard* has fared better, surviving her three sisters, *Alf Everard*, *Ethel Everard* and *Fred Everard* and still in commission in 2003. All four of these large barges were, like the *Greenhithe*, products of the Fellowes Shipyard. The *'Will'* and *'Alf'* built just a couple of years after the *Greenhithe*, the *'Ethel'* and *'Fred'* the year after that. The *Will Everard* was engined in 1950 but retained her full sailing gear until she came out of trade in December 1966. Re-named *Will*, by the mid 1970s she was a 'hospitality' vessel for Overseas Containers Ltd and passed into P & O hands in 1986. After many years use to heighten the profile of P & O operations, she was sold to her long serving Master, Sue Harrison, in whose ownership at the Acorn Shipyard, Rochester, she remains today.

The wooden barge *Thalatta* was always well maintained by R. & W. Paul at their own Dock End Shipyard by the entrance to Ipswich Dock. She survives in active commission, approaching her centenary, having been operated for nearly forty years by the East Coast Sail Trust, enabling disadvantaged youngsters and others to experience life afloat under sail.

The 121 years old *George Smeed* is still afloat at Maldon where she has been undergoing an extensive and on-going rebuild over a period approaching three decades. There are hopes that she will soon be rigged out and underway.

If Ivan's experiences were anything to go by, the *Saltcote Belle* was well past her prime when last in trade. She was sold for conversion to a yacht barge in 1951 and had a number of owners in the years which followed. The *Saltcote Belle* successfully raced in the barge matches during the 1960s, proving the old Maldon bargemen were correct in saying she was 'a fast bit of wood'. Eventually the barge became a houseboat at Tollesbury, her sailing gear having been sold to re-rig the *Felix*. Finally her hogged hull was abandoned in the nearby saltings to become derelict. Little remains to be seen now of the old *Saltcote Belle*, but one of her bow rails, with her name carved in a banner, was saved and is now displayed in the bar of a waterside pub.

Like the *George Smeed* and *Saltcote Belle*, the *Lady Helen* also spent many years in the ownership of Francis & Gilders, the Colchester barge owners. She was built by Gill and Sons at Rochester in 1902 as a medium sized coasting barge, but in later years was useful as being just able to navigate under the low bridges to reach East Mills at Colchester. The *Lady Helen* was motorised in 1952 but retained most of her sailing gear. Her sail plan was later further reduced and after the mainsail blew to ribbons she traded under power alone within the Thames Estuary limits, fitted with a small mast and derrick. As with the *George Smeed*, the *Lady Helen* was also sold to Brown & Son of Chelmsford and used along with other old barge hulls for lightering timber from Baltic ships, anchored in the Maldon River, to Heybridge Basin. By the mid-1960s the sea lock chamber of the Basin was lengthened to admit the timber carrying ships and the sailing barge hulls became redundant. The *Lady Helen* was sold for £500 to a private buyer with the intention of moving her by road to the River Cam near Cambridge for conversion into a restaurant. The idea fell through and the barge was sold again to become a houseboat at Maldon, then later moored by the sea wall close to the lock entrance of Heybridge Basin. Twenty-five years since coming out of the Basin, the *Lady Helen* was placed on Cook's blocks at Maldon where her stern disintegrated. The remains of the stern and her rudder were dumped in the barge graveyard near the end of the Maldon promenade, the remainder of her hull moved alongside the derelict *Charles Burley* lying by the sea wall between Heybridge Basin and Herrings Point.

Under the London & Rochester Trading Company house flag, the steel *Atrato*, originally a sailing barge from the Wivenhoe shipyard of Forrestt & Sons in 1898, was engined as early as 1923 for the upper Medway trade. She is now moored at Battersea where her owner lives aboard, slowly putting her back to sailing condition.

Goldsmith's *Cambria* was not so lucky. Built in 1899 by Fay at Southampton to one of the standard barge designs pioneered by her owners, she also came under the Crescent flag of the London & Rochester Trading Company following the take over of the London firm. She was stripped for lightering duties by 1951 and was broken up in 1953.

Some two dozen sailing barges remain in commission, mainly kept in their traditional waters. Despite the fact that this is less than one per cent of the number that traded a century ago, it is a unique 'fleet' of sailing cargo carriers from an era long gone. Today their 'cargoes' are people - sailing barge enthusiasts, corporate business guests, photographers and bird-watchers, instead of the wheat or stack of straw that filled the holds in 'trade'.

Pam Hazelton, Barry Pearce and Richard Walsh

PHOTOGRAPHS

The pictures which have been included in this book feature many of the craft and people around which this story is woven. Others are included because they are typical of the period, although in that context, some may be a little earlier or later as photography around the docks in wartime was prohibited, and immediately after the war film was difficult to obtain. Some of the photographs included are from poor quality originals, or have deteriorated with the passage of time, but are included because of their particular relevance to the text.

These photographs are mainly from private collections, and the book is much the better for their inclusion, so sincere thanks go to all who have made them available to reproduce here.

Every endeavour has been made to correctly and comprehensively identify photograph sources, but the origins and provenance of some are obscure. Where the word Photo appears, the name which follows is believed to be that of the photographer. In each case, the current provider is listed last. The photographs are identified by page number and position.

PAGE	SOURCE
5:	St. Lawrence Studios, Ipswich; Pam Hazelton Collection.
6:	Graham Dent Collection.
8:	Photo. - Daphne Oliver; Richard Smith Collection.
12:	Fred Cooper Collection; Ray Rush Collection.
19:	Fred Cooper Collection; Ray Rush Collection.
22:	Photo. - Arthur Bennett; Richard Walsh Collection.
31:	Fred Cooper Collection; Ray Rush Collection.
34:	Andrew Haig Collection.
41:	World Ship Society; Graham Dent Collection.
46 top:	Museum in Docklands - P.L.A. Collection.
46 bottom:	Museum in Docklands - P.L.A. Collection.
53:	World Ship Society; Graham Dent Collection.
56:	Museum in Docklands - P.L.A. Collection.
61:	Photo. - Philip Kershaw; Fred Cooper Collection; Ray Rush Collection.
63:	Tony Farnham Collection.
64:	Hervey Benham Collection; Ron Green Collection.

67:	Photo. - T. Rayner; Fred Cooper Collection; Ray Rush Collection.
71:	Hervey Benham Collection; Ron Green Collection.
74:	Tony Farnham Collection.
77:	Photo. - R. Stimpson Jnr; Fred Cooper Collection; Ray Rush Collection.
80:	Photo. - Mary Love; Paddy O'Driscoll Collection; Barry Pearce Collection.
82:	Fred Cooper Collection; Ray Rush Collection.
86:	Photo. - Philip Kershaw; Fred Cooper Collection; Ray Rush Collection.
87:	Graham Dent Collection.
89:	Photo. - G. Osbon; Rick Hogben Collection.
92:	Unilever Plc., Colman's Archive.
94:	Photo. - Pan-Aero Pictures; Bob Smith Collection; Delia Smith Collection.
97:	Photo. - E. N. Naylor; Ken Garrett Collection.
103:	Tony Farnham Collection.
106:	Fred Cooper Collection; Ray Rush Collection.
108:	Tony Farnham Collection.
111:	Duncan Francis Collection.
113:	Pam Hazelton Collection.
116:	Photo. - Douglas Went; Hervey Benham Collection; Ron Green Collection.
120:	Pam Hazelton Collection.
122:	Fred Cooper Collection; Ray Rush Collection.
124:	Tony Farnham Collection.
127:	Pam Hazelton Collection.
128:	Photo. - Roger Finch; Fred Cooper Collection; Ray Rush Collection.
130:	Pam Hazelton Collection.
131:	Photo. - C. C. (Jack) Beazley.
133 top:	Island History Trust postcard; Tony Farnham Collection.
133 bottom:	Photochrom Co. Ltd.; Tony Farnham Collection.
138:	Photo. - Douglas Went; Tony Farnham Collection.
141:	Peter Pearson Collection.
142:	The Prior Associated Companies Archive.
149:	Tony Farnham Collection.
153:	Photo. - Ray Rush.
157:	Photo. - Carter; Lincolnshire County Council, Gainsborough Library.
158:	Sheila Roberts Collection.
162:	Barry Pearce Collection
165:	Photo. - Charles Hill; Ken Garrett Collection.
167:	Photo. - Barry Pearce.
168 top:	Barry Pearce Collection
168 bottom:	Photo. - Paddy O'Driscoll.

Vessels names are shown in *italics* throughout

Index prepared by Milla Hills
Indexing Specialists (U.K.) Limited
202 Church Road
Hove
East Sussex BN3 2DJ

176